LETTERS
THAT
SELL

LETTERS THAT SELL

EDWARD W. WERZ

CB
CONTEMPORARY
BOOKS
CHICAGO

Library of Congress Cataloging-in-Publication Data

Werz, Edward W.
  Letters that sell.

  1. Sales letters.   I. Title.
HF5730.W47   1987   808'.066651   87-20064
  ISBN 0-8092-4684-8 (pbk.)

To Janice. For Everything.

Copyright © 1987 by Edward W. Werz
All rights reserved
Published by Contemporary Books, Inc.
Two Prudential Plaza, Chicago, Illinois 60601-6790
Manufactured in the United States of America
International Standard Book Number: 0-8092-4684-8

CONTENTS

Introduction

The value of sales letters as a powerful marketing tool cannot be overstated. Sales letters work. They answer customer questions, pique the prospect's interest, turn inquiries into orders, and, most of all, sell. And when they sell, they sell irresistibly and efficiently. Sales letters may, in fact, be the most effective medium available to many advertisers because of four very special qualities.

First, sales letters are personal. They are the only medium, excepting the more costly sales visit and telemarketing call, where the advertiser communicates directly with the prospect in a personal manner. People enjoy receiving personal mail. That's because the letter's news may be good or reveal an important opportunity. Sales letters are one-to-one messages. The recipient knows that the letter is for his or her sole consideration. The sales message is therefore perceived as a personal, intimate, and exclusive offer. When people are shown special attention, they feel flattered and react positively. Sales letters, by the nature of the medium, are received as openly as any advertising approach.

Second, sales letters are not intimidating. Unlike personal and telephone sales calls, where pressure is often applied to the prospect, the sales letter is pressure-free. A reader who is not interested simply throws the letter away. This freedom allows the prospect to examine sales letters without fear of arm twisting.

Third, when the prospect opens a sales letter it holds his or her complete attention for a few seconds. This provides the marketer with an exceptional opportunity to present and construct a strong, cohesive, and in-depth sales argument without any distractions. Controlling the prospect's exclusive attention is a rare and advantageous occurrence in selling.

Fourth, and possibly most important, sales letters can reach the prime prospect population to which the product or service can be sold. Most media, including print, television, public relations, billboard, and radio, can be described as shotgun advertising. Although sellers use demographics, much of the audience has no particular need for the product or service. The message and advertising budget are, in fact, wasted on these people. Sales letters, on the other hand, are sent *only* to the prospects with the best chance of buying: those on precise, targeted mailing lists. If the sender takes advantage of a good mailing list, there is virtually no waste.

Because of these four qualities, well-written sales letters consistently produce better results than most alternative media. If you use sales letters already, this book will help you increase their effectiveness. And if you have not yet tried sales letters, you will quickly learn their special power.

How to Use This Book

Letters That Sell offers you a large selection of model sales letters covering many of the most common selling situations. While you can use many of the letters as they are (with substitutions of your information), the best use of the letters is as a guide. Before writing your letter, read the appropriate section introduction. Then find the model letter that best approximates your particular sales situation. Closely review the notations to the left of the letter. The notations provide you with the sequence of the sales presentation. In addition, they highlight selling suggestions and strategies. By following this handy format, you will find it easy to pen persuasive letters that sell.

Sales Letters: A Science and an Art

The Science of Writing Sales Letters

Effective sales letters combine creativity and scientific execution. By following a number of precise rules, tested and proved over decades of experience in sales promotion, you can draft letters that will produce excellent results. Not every letter you write will work, but if you follow a scientific approach, more of your sales letters will be winning letters.

Effective sales letters have four elements in common. These elements follow a logical sequence that leads the prospect to a point where a decision to purchase is probable. Here they are:

1. Begin by capturing the prospect's attention.

2. Next, show a need and answer that need with the benefits of the product or service.

3. Convince the prospect with a special offer or by establishing credibility and reliability.

4. Finally, ask for the order or other action.

Capture the Prospect's Attention

If a letter doesn't get the reader's attention, it is never read and no action occurs. Most sales letters do not get read; they are thrown away without ever being considered. Why? Because the writer is unaware that the decision to read or not to read is made in the first five seconds. Pick up a sales letter and count to five as you study it. Although you cannot read much of it in that short time, you develop a strong impression. That impression is what the decision of whether to continue reading is based upon. What could make a prospect decide, in five seconds, to read a letter? Consider these factors:

- *The salutation.* Does it establish a bond or rapport with the reader? If it does, there is an excellent chance the prospect will read further.

- *The headline or opening sentence.* Does it interest, intrigue, excite, provoke, enlighten, or arouse the reader? Good strong openings invite continued reading.

- *The format.* Is it a form letter? Or is the letter personalized? Does the letter have an unusual look or novelty enclosure? The more the letter's format holds the reader's interest, the more likely it is to be read.

- *The envelope and letterhead.* Is the envelope individually typed and stamped? Or is it addressed with a mailing label and bulk-mailed? Is the letter typed on a well-designed, quality letterhead? Or is it a photocopy? The more personal and professional the letter looks, the more carefully it will be considered.

Of the four factors discussed, the most powerful is the headline or opening sentence. The opening sentence must attract and hold the reader's attention. If the reader is not intrigued, the letter is not read, and no product is sold. Types of sentences that work include the following:

- *Sentences that make a challenge—* "I dare you to find a ___ that costs less!"

- *Sentences that ask a question—* "Have you ever dreamed of owning a vacation home?"

- *Sentences that make a personal connection—*"Let me tell you about the biggest mistake I ever made."

- *Sentences that make an offer—*"Get two ___s for the price of one."

- *Sentences that promise something for free—*"I've enclosed a FREE pencil with your name handsomely imprinted to show you the strong impression you can make with low-cost, specialty advertising."

- *Sentences that make the reader feel important—*"If you receive this letter, you are one in a hundred."

- *Sentences that present something new or different—*"Announcing the first talking computer for home use!"

First impressions really count when it comes to sales letters. The writer should spend as much time making sure the letter passes the five-second test as he or she spends writing the rest of the letter.

Showing a Need and Answering It
Why do people buy? People take actions, which include buying, in order

to satisfy their basic needs. When we are born, our needs are about as basic as they can get. We need to eat, drink, stay warm and clean, and receive stimulation. These are the requirements of *survival*. We are led by our instincts to act in ways that keep us alive. For instance, a baby cries if it is hungry. As we get older, we still behave according to our basic need to survive, but our actions are more complex. We might, for example, amplify the need for warmth with the desire to own a duplex condominium and amplify the need for stimulation with the need for a meaningful relationship. As adults we buy not only to satisfy basic survival needs, but for many reasons:

- For pride
- To earn money
- To save money
- For comfort
- To reduce work
- To save time
- For prestige
- For health
- To avoid pain
- For praise
- To be popular

- To attract a mate
- For pleasure
- For recognition
- To live longer
- To avoid embarrassment
- To avoid trouble
- To take advantage of opportunities
- To protect reputation
- To enhance individuality
- To avoid criticism
- For safety
- To emulate others
- To satisfy appetite
- To have possessions
- To be accepted
- To protect loved ones
- To gratify curiosity
- To look young, beautiful
- For sexual satisfaction

Show the need for the product or service immediately after grabbing the reader's attention. Then answer that need through the benefits derived from the product or service. Some examples follow.

The Need: To look younger.

Identifying the Need: Most Americans are overweight. Extra pounds not only make us feel uncomfortable, they make us look older! You've seen it time and time again. As soon as someone loses weight, that person looks younger.

Answering the Need: The PoundsAway Diet System lets you lose weight quickly and safely. After only seven days, you'll look and feel younger.

The Need: To protect your family.

Identifying the Need: More people lose their lives from fires in their home than by any other form of home accident. A majority of these terrible deaths result from smoke inhalation.

Answering the Need: You can protect your family from the danger of smoke inhalation with the AlertFirst Smoke Alarm System. It warns you with a loud, piercing siren when there is smoke in your home. Even if you are asleep, you are awakened in time to escape to safety.

The Need: To reduce work.

Identifying the Need: Do you put in a full day's work and go home feeling that you haven't accomplished anything? Nothing can be as disconcerting as feeling overwhelmed on the job.

Answering the Need: Now, you can accomplish more without working harder! How? By learning three practical principles of time management described in the important report, *Time and Work,* available to you today at a special price.

Often a sales organization sells the same product over and over again to the same account. An example of this is a cosmetics company selling department stores an established line of makeup, or a confectionery manufacturer selling a successful brand of candy to distributors. In cases like these, sales letters have previously addressed the need, so new sales points must be made. Some possible approaches are:

- Citing the successful sales history of the product

- Announcing market statistics showing customer preference and satisfaction

- Describing a new promotion, point-of-purchase display, or package that should help increase sales

- Other original sales messages that may benefit the customer

Convince the Prospect
The letter has held the prospect's

attention, identified a human need, and answered it through the product's or service's benefits. Now it is time to persuade the reader to get off the fence and decide to buy. This is done by making a special offer or allaying the prospect's doubts with evidence of your excellence. Some possible special offers include:

- *Price*—Half price, two for one, *x* percent off, introductory price, final clearance, take 20 percent off, discounted to $y, etc.

- *Trial*—Free trial offer, 30-day no-risk offer, no-money trial, free trial subscription, yours to examine . . . free, etc.

- *Free*—Free sample, free refill when you buy _____, free gift, send for free information, as an extra bonus, _____ free, order now and get a free _____, etc.

- *Guarantee*—Fully guaranteed, money-back guarantee, full-year warranty, 30-day no-risk guarantee, your money back if you are not completely satisfied, etc.

The best way to satisfy doubts about the company or the product or service is to cite evidence of reliability. Most effective are testimonials from third parties. These include letters of satisfaction, testimonial letters, quotations from buyers, reviews in consumer publications, awards won, ratings, statistics, and other objective material. Offering to provide the phone numbers of satisfied customers also can be extremely convincing.

Sometimes, you may have additional information that may help the prospect's business, but not necessarily lead to a sale of your product or service. By offering this information to the prospect, either within the letter or as an enclosure, you establish your concern for the prospect's needs. By providing something extra, you convey your company's professionalism and project the image of a credible and reliable organization. You can be sure that your future sales letters will be read and seriously considered.

Asking for the Order
The last element in the sales letter is the simple, clear, and direct request for the order. If the prospect does not order now, the order is probably lost forever. Therefore, *keep it simple*. Avoid long, complicated instructions or explanations. Instead, tell the reader what to do in one or two short sentences. Whenever possible, urge the prospect to act immediately. Here are some examples:

- "Return the reply card now because

this special offer will be honored for 10 days only."

- "We have reserved a _____ for you for 30 days only. At this remarkable price they are sure to go fast, so please call the toll-free number and order now!"

- "Drop the postage-free reply card in the mail now, and we'll rush you the free information. There's no obligation, so mail it today!"

The P.S.

The postscript can reinforce the request for the order. Studies have shown that often the P.S. is the first part of the letter that is read. If it is not read first, then it is read last. Either way, the P.S. carries a great deal of weight. When a sales letter has presented a strong sales argument based on a single product feature or offer, it is often advisable to present a new, enticing sales point in the postscript. Where the letter has set forth many sales points, an effective use of the P.S. is to reinforce the most powerful argument. Remember, however, to use the P.S. only when you do have something new to add, whether it is a new feature or offer or a new way of supporting your major sales theme.

Once you master the science of writing sales letters, you will find them easy to write. The system will become second nature to you, and you'll become comfortable enough to bend a rule now and then. You'll automatically think of your sales goals and how they coincide with the needs of your clients or prospects.

The Art of Writing Sales Letters

Writing effective business letters is an art as well as a science because really good letters transcend the ordinary. They are truly creative messages that capture the reader's interest, hold it, and build a strong desire to want the product or service. Anyone can be creative in letter writing, although many people freeze when they try to be creative. Here are some suggestions to help you become more in tune with your creative self:

- Always imagine yourself as a creative individual. The more you think of yourself as a creative person, the more you will free your imagination to be innovative.

- Avoid being your own censor. Let all your ideas flow without prejudging them. Write them down as you think of them. Try to generate as many new ideas as possible. Even if the idea is not original, include it. Often two, three, or more old ideas combine to form a novel concept.

- Become obsessed with the problem or opportunity. Think about it as much as possible in as many situations as you can. Think about it when driving, after seeing a movie, while in a bookstore, wherever you can. By considering the problem in many different environments, you increase the variety of sensory information you receive. This stimulation may evoke new ideas and relationships.

- Build a swipe file. Clip and collect clever magazine ads, direct-mail packages, and sales letters, whether they relate to your project or not. Review the file while thinking about the problem. The ideas will begin to flow fast and furiously.

- Do some informal market research. Ask your friends and business associates what they think. Find out what features interest them. Most important, find out how the product or service impresses them emotionally.

- When everything you try leads you to a dead end, step away from the problem. Play a round of golf or a game of tennis. Take a short vacation, walk on the beach, do whatever relaxes you. Try not to think about the problem at all. Often, the most creative solutions or approaches will jump into your mind at times of complete relaxation.

Your originality and unique perspective underlie the art of letter writing. We are all born with creative talent. We can use it successfully in our letter writing by approaching the writing task with a relaxed, open, confident, and enthusiastic attitude. Just say you can . . . and you will!

Other Considerations for Writers

A Word About Honesty

For sales letters to work, the reader must be convinced of the credibility of the offer. As soon as a doubt about the writer's sincerity arises, all hope for a sale is lost. A common mistake in many sales letters is an exaggeration of the benefits. A straightforward statement of the benefits will outperform an overzealous one every time. Therefore, present a candid account of your product or service. Your honesty will come through, and your letters will be more effective.

Writing Style

Because sales letters are a personal form of communication, the style of the writing can generally be less formal than in other types of business correspondence. However, each particular situation should be evaluated on its own merits. An example of an informal letter would be one sent to a long-time customer with whom you have developed a personal relationship. A less personal, more formal letter would go to a purchasing agent of a company with which you have never done business.

You will find that many of the letters in this book use an informal, personal style. The style is similar to that used in normal conversation. They are written from an "I" rather than a "we" point of view. Contractions such as *you're* and *you'll* are frequently used to maintain a conversational tone.

Most letters end with the standard business close, "Sincerely yours." When the letter is friendlier or more intimate, an informal close, "Cordially yours," is used. Goodwill letters and certain letters to customers and salespeople use the informal close. Feel free to use other informal closes ("Best," "Regards") if you feel they are more suited to your audience.

Additional Tips for Writing Letters That Sell

- Keep the sentences short and to the point.

- Short paragraphs are more inviting than long ones. If you keep paragraphs brief, you're more likely to keep the reader involved.

- Use emotional words rather than conceptual ones. For example, replace the word *gratifying* with the word *fun*.

- Underline words and sentences for emphasis.

- Use all CAPITAL LETTERS, **bold type**, or *italics* for headlines and motivating words like *free, now, limited*, and *new*.

- Explain the reason for the letter in the first or second paragraph.

- Avoid humor unless you are very sure it will be effective and that it could not possibly offend anyone.

- Indent whole paragraphs to make them stand out. This works well for special offers or important sales points.

- Try to concentrate on one main sales argument. More than one can cause confusion.

- Use bullets (•) or asterisks (*) to draw attention to specific points.

- Repeat the key selling point at least twice in the letter. Say it in a different manner so that, if it was not understood the first time, it will be the second time.

- Before using novelty enclosures or attention grabbers like colored stationery, consider the image you wish to project.

Here are two examples of sales letters. One letter is written poorly, ignoring the principles of effective sales-letter writing. Although the poor letter was written to be ineffective, it is surprisingly similar to many letters that come across one's desk every day. The good letter, on the other hand, is an example of the art and science of writing sales letters that work. It grabs the reader's attention with an intriguing opening. Next it identifies a need and answers that need through the benefits of the product. The reader is persuaded to act because of low price and lack of risk. Finally, the prospect is asked to take action and told how to do so. The two letters differ dramatically in their power to compel.

Sample Poor Letter

Opening is impersonal.

No need is established, and no benefit mentioned.

The reader is probably not interested in learning the history of the company.

The sales message is not specific enough. One product should be described and marketed.

The letter asks the reader to do work without any apparent benefit. It is asking the impossible.

Again, too vague. How, when, and about what will the reader be contacted?

Dear Resident:

We are writing you to tell you about the Mutual Life Company and its services.

Mutual Life was founded in 1902 by William Hunter. Our company has grown steadily and today is the third largest insurance company in the Northeast. Our assets exceed a billion dollars. In fact, one in every five homeowners in the Northeast is insured with a Mutual Life policy.

Mutual Life provides a full range of financial products and services. We know that one of these products will answer your insurance needs.

But to find out which is ideal for you, we need your help. Please complete the short questionnaire and return it to Mutual Life.

We will contact you with complete information and recommendations.

Thank you for this opportunity to serve you.

Sincerely yours,

Sample Good Letter

Using the reader's name opens on a personal note.	Dear _____:
An intriguing question captures the reader's attention.	<u>Do you ever lose sleep worrying about your family's future?</u>
The product is immediately presented as a solution to the reader's need or problem.	You could sleep peacefully tonight if you knew your family was protected with a Mutual Life Mortgage Insurance Policy.
The product is explained directly and concisely. The emotional benefit is reinforced.	This policy instantly pays the balance of your home mortgage upon your death. Your family's future would be secure.
The problem is amplified to build desire.	Today, with the high cost of housing, mortgage insurance is a necessity. That's because too many families find, upon the loss of a loved one, that they must give up the home they cherish.
The product is linked to the reader's feelings.	<u>Owning mortgage insurance is an expression of concern for your family.</u>
The reader is told exactly how to take action.	Find out today how inexpensive this valuable protection can be. I've enclosed a short application form for you to fill out. It takes only five minutes and does not obligate you in any manner. As soon as I receive it, I will call you with Mutual's low, low rates.

A benefit of acting quickly is emphasized.

We can have your application approved and your protection in effect within seven days. So, please mail it now. The sooner you do, the sooner your family will have this important safeguard.

Sincerely yours,

The postscript reminds the reader that immediate action will bring peace of mind.

P.S. Remember, if you send in the application today, you'll sleep better tonight!

CHAPTER 1

DIRECT-SELL LETTERS

The measure of a good direct-sell letter is in its ability to motivate the reader to act. The action might be to place an order, fill out a survey, request a brochure, accept a trial subscription, visit a store, or a score of other behaviors ultimately leading to a sale.

Direct-sell letters that work follow four scientific steps. First, the reader's interest is won with an attention-getting opening. Second, a need is identified and answered through the features and benefits of the product. Third, the reader is convinced with a special offer or demonstration of credibility. And fourth, the reader is asked to order or take other action.

Let us look at the second step a little more closely. Probably the most common mistake made in sales-letter writing is made in this critical stage of the letter. The mistake is to focus on the features of the product or service rather than the benefits. When a sales letter describes only features, it is not answering the needs, concerns, and problems of the prospect. If you have a toothache, for instance, you want to hear about how quickly and painlessly the dentist will relieve your pain, not where his or her drill was manufactured.

Here are some examples of the ineffective focus on features and the effective focus on benefits. Notice the difference.

Focus on Features: These running shorts are made of 100 percent nylon.

Focus on Benefits: These running shorts are made 100 percent nylon so they will dry quickly when you perspire.

Focus on Features: The shampoo comes in a handy plastic bottle.

Focus on Benefits: The shampoo comes in a handy plastic bottle so it won't break even if dropped in the shower. It's perfectly safe, even for your children to use.

Focus on Features: The pen has a special cartridge so you can write in three colors.

Focus on Benefits: The special cartridge lets you write in three colors so you don't have to change pens to highlight or color-code. You save time and effort!

Focus on Features: All models include a sun roof.

Focus on Benefits: All models include a sun roof, providing you with the fun and freedom of a convertible and the safety and security of a hard top.

Focus on Features: We're open 24 hours a day.

Focus on Benefits: We're open 24 hours a day so you can visit us for breakfast, lunch, dinner, or a snack. Whenever you're hungry, we're ready to serve you.

Letter Selling a Consumer Product

Salutation qualifies reader. (Here, notice how reader is given sympathy).

Dear Backache Sufferer:

Get the reader's attention by showing a powerful need.

<u>You no longer have to endure the incredible pain and discomfort of back spasms.</u>

Show how your product answers the need.

Thousands of backache sufferers like you have found soothing relief with Back-A-Matt, the low-cost, scientifically designed air mattress for people with back problems.

Establish yourself as an authority by providing facts the reader will identify with.

Poor back support from ordinary bedding can cause or aggravate back muscle spasms. That's why so many people wake up in the morning with back pain.

Explain how your products deliver the benefits you promise.

Back-A-Matt is an inflatable mattress with specially designed inner cells that conform gently to your body, providing firm support. As you bend or turn, Back-A-Matt adjusts to your individual contours. You'll sleep in comfort and wake pain-free and energized when you sleep on Back-A-Matt.

Sell the benefit of low price.

If Back-A-Matt sold for $300, it would be a great value. But its price is not $300 or $200 or even $100. Back-A-Matt is yours for the remarkable price of $89 delivered! And that's for a queen-size mattress.

Provide the details the reader will need before a decision can be made.

Back-A-Matt is constructed of sturdy vinyl, is water-resistant, and inflates in minutes using an ordinary hair dryer. And it's as comfortable on the floor as it is on box springs.

Use a money-back guarantee to remove all doubt.	Back-A-Matt is offered to you for a 10-day free trial. Just call the toll-free number or return the order card tody. If you are not totally satisfied, return Back-A-Matt and owe nothing. If, however, you find Back-A-Matt to be all we say it is and decide to keep it, you will be billed only $89.
Reinforce the benefit and tell the reader what he or she must do.	Freedom from pain for only $89 . . . amazing! Don't delay. Order your Back-A-Matt now while supplies last.
	Sincerely yours,

Letter Selling a Business Product

Salutation qualifies reader and shows that you understand his or her busy schedule. A question gets the reader's attention and establishes a need.

Dear Busy Executive:

Do You Waste Valuable Time Keeping Schedules Up-to-Date?

Promise the solution to the need.

Now you can arrange and rearrange schedules in seconds with an ingenious business tool used by hundreds of thousands of successful executives.

Answer the need with the product's features and benefits.

Magnetic Scheduling Boards hang on your wall like a picture and provide you with an up-to-the-minute picture of your entire operation at a glance. And best of all, you make changes in seconds just by moving magnets. Your schedules are always current, and you are always totally in control of even the most hectic, complicated work load.

Describe additional benefits.

In addition, Magnetic Control Boards help you in the following ways:

- They help you communicate with your staff, as all scheduling information is clearly visible.

- They help you coordinate and plan multiple projects.

- They make it easy for you to set and meet objectives and goals.

- They assist you in prioritizing assignments and organizing work flow.

Make a special offer.	Because we're so sure a Magnetic Control Board is just what you need to save you valuable time, we'd like to make you a special offer.
Explain the offer.	We'll send you our most popular model, complete with all the magnets and colored-paper inserts you'll need, FREE for 30 days. Try it out. If you decide it's as helpful as we've said it is, pay only $99.95. That's a savings of over $25.00 off the regular price. If, however, you decide you do not wish to keep the board, simply return it to us. No questions will be asked.
Ask for immediate action. Use the limited offer to create a feeling of urgency.	Don't wait. You have only 10 days to take advantage of this special offer. Fill out the postage-paid reply card and mail it now!
Reinforce the need, as well as the need to act now.	You owe it to yourself and your career to try this business efficiency product . . . so act today!
	Sincerely yours,
Promise free information as an added incentive.	P.S. When you order, we'll also send you our FREE guide to scheduling. It contains dozens of important, time-saving tips.

Letter Selling a Consumer Service

Salutation qualifies prospect. (Notice the positive message when using the word *lover*.)

Dear Dog Lover:

Use a surprising fact to get the reader's attention.

When you give your dog a bath, you may be <u>actually causing it harm!</u>

Develop the need.

It's true! Most dog owners either irritate their dog's skin or create a dry-skin condition by overbathing or using a harsh or too concentrated shampoo. That's why dogs often scratch more after a bath than before one.

Show how your service answers the need.

Now, with our special service, your dog can have a bath guaranteed to be both cleansing and soothing.

Describe how your service delivers the benefits promised.

We're Fido-Wash. Our mobile pet salon will come to your home, and we'll give your pet a safe shampoo that will also protect your dog from fleas.

Make an introductory offer to motivate the reader to act.

As a special introduction, we're offering you our normal $19.95 deluxe shampoo with flea treatment for only $9.95.

Ask for the order while emphasizing the benefits.

Take this moment to call us to set up a visit. See for yourself how a professional shampoo will keep your dog healthy and contented.

Reinforce the limited nature of the offer.

We may never make an offer like this again, so call us now!

Sincerely yours,

Use the postscript to present another selling point.

P.S. Studies have shown that regularly bathed dogs live healthier and longer lives. Give Fido-Wash a try!

Letter Selling a Business Service

Salutation qualifies reader.

Dear Comptroller:

A question piques the reader's interest.

Are You Spending More Money Trying to Collect Delinquent Accounts Than You Are Getting Back?

The need is elaborated.

Many companies have realized that when they add up the costs for in-house collection personnel, telephone calls, mailings, and miscellaneous expenses, they find their collection operation is actually *losing* money.

The need is answered.

Now, you can have a professional collection service handle every detail of the collection process and get you more money back at a lower cost to you than your current operation.

A secondary benefit is explained.

What's more, we guarantee you that we will collect more money than you do. That's becuase collections are our only business. After 15 years in collections, we've developed a systematic approach that produces excellent results.

The feature of no-risk becomes an important benefit.

Best of all, there is no fee for our service. We are paid a percentage of what we collect. If we are not effective, we don't get paid!

Establish credibility.

I've enclosed a list of companies in your area that we work with. Please call them and ask them about our service. Their satisfaction is a testimony to our professionalism.

Make a special offer and emphasize the urgency of acting quickly.

As a special introduction to our service, we are offering you our service for three months at half our normal percentage. But to receive this special price, you must return the reply card within the next two weeks. After June 1, this special rate will no longer be available.

Tell the reader what action to take. (Also notice that the second sentence both presumes cooperation and serves to further motivate the reader by suggesting he or she *deserves* the service.)

So, mail the reply card today. We look forward to helping you collect more of the money that is owed you.

Sincerely yours,

Reinforce an important benefit with facts or statistics.

P.S. A recent survey of our customers indicated that we increased their collection of delinquent accounts by 30 percent. We can do the same for you!

Letter Selling a Subscription

Salutation qualifies reader.	Dear Golfer:
Promise a benefit that the reader will truly desire. (Note that here, fulfilling the need and capturing the reader's attention are done at the same time.)	You can knock 10 strokes off your golf game this season by subscribing to the revolutionary new golf magazine, *Beginning Golfer*!
Add a second benefit—saving money.	And, with the special charter offer described later, save 50 percent off the regular subscription price.
Explain in detail how the publication will do all it promises. Tell specifically what it will contain.	*Beginning Golfer* is the first fully instructional golf magazine written specifically for the beginner. Each month, the finest teaching professionals take you step by step through the fundamentals of golf. Every issue covers an essential aspect of the golf game in detail. You'll find practical instructions, revealing photo essays, informative question-and-answer features, fascinating tips and secrets, and much, much more.
Substantiate and add credibility to the promise with proof or an example.	Before it was ever offered for sale, *Beginning Golfer* was used by golf pros as a teaching aid at hundreds of golf clinics. They have seen its instructional value proved again and again. Now, it's your turn to take advantage of this unusually effective, innovative golf magazine.
Promote the special offer and ask for action. State the discount in as many different ways as possible.	The regular subscription price for *Beginning Golfer* is $25.00. But, for a limited time, you can have a full year's subscription for only $12.50. That's 50 percent off! We make this

special charter subscription offer only once. It will not be available again. So be sure you order today.

Minimize the risk with a guarantee and reinforce the benefit.

If, for any reason, you are not satisfied with *Beginning Golfer* or do not see a marked improvement in your game, you can cancel your subscription and receive a full, no-questions-asked refund. That is how positive we are that *Beginning Golfer* will cut strokes off your game.

Ask for the order one last time and remind the reader again of the product benefit.

So order today! As soon as you do, you'll be on your way to the lowest golf scores you've ever shot.

Sincerely yours,

Add an extra incentive for ordering.

P.S. When you subscribe, you receive a dozen FREE golf balls. That's a $24.00 value!

Letter Selling a Travel Investment

Salutation qualifies prospect.

Dear Vacationer:

Begin with an exciting offer to entice the prospect. (The word *escape* shows the need to get away from a hectic work schedule.)

Escape to tropical Aruba for six exciting days and five fabulous nights as our guest.

Present the offer.

That's right, we'll pay for your accommodations and two meals a day. All you pay for is the airfare, and we can get you a special rate of only $295 per person round trip.

Anticipate the prospect's skepticism by describing the reason for this special offer.

What's the catch? There is none. We manage the Aruba Club, a new luxury resort located on one of the finest beaches in the world. Most of the people who stay with us purchase one of our villas as a vacation home. Our offer is the only way we promote our resort. As we like to say, "A stay is worth a thousand ads."

Enumerate the features of the resort.

Here are some of the sensational features of the Aruba Club:

- Olympic-size swimming pool
- Health center
- Three restaurants
- Tennis and golf
- Casino
- Beautiful villas located on the beach, each with a spacious balcony overlooking the ocean.

Sell the benefits of the investment.	Your only obligation is to take our delightful, one-hour Resort Home Tour. You'll learn how owning a vacation resort home can be an excellent, appreciating investment as well as a money-saving tax shelter.
Provide the prospect with a reason to act quickly.	After this mailing, there will be more people interested in this hard-to-believe vacation offer than accommodations available, so call us immediately.
Promise more information when the prospect calls.	When you call, we'll make reservations for you and send you our full-color brochure. You must be over 21 years of age, and this offer is limited to two people per party.
Tell the reader what action to take and reinforce the limited availability.	Call for your reservations today, as space is limited and offered on a first come, first serve basis.
	Sincerely yours,
Provide one more incentive for the prospect to act.	P.S. When you call, we'll also send you, FREE, two tropical T-shirts you can wear on the beach!

Letter Selling an Educational Seminar

Salutation qualifies reader. (Notice the positive feeling conveyed using the word *lover*.)

Dear Crafts Lover:

Open with the powerful promise of benefit that meets a perceived need (here, financial gain).

You can now turn your handicraft hobby into a profitable part-time business.

Describe the benefit in tangible terms.

Many crafts lovers like you agree—there's no more enjoyable way to make money. Imagine earning hundreds of dollars a month doing what you would normally do for the fun of it.

Entice the reader with the promise of an easy-to-learn system.

There are six easy steps for turning a crafts hobby into a money-making part-time business. And you can learn them all by enrolling in our exciting course, "Turning Your Hobby into Your Crafts Business."

Describe the seminar, using concrete examples of topics covered.

You'll learn from experts who run successful craft businesses. Important topics include:

- Avoiding Common Mistakes That Can Ruin You

- Six Ways to Get Free Advertising

- Discount Suppliers and Where to Find Them

- Tax-Saving Ideas That Put Money in Your Pocket

- Mail Order Marketing

- And much more!

Urge the reader to act.	So don't delay! Send in the reply card now, and we'll send you a special brochure describing the course in more detail.
Offer free information as an incentive to act and tell the reader exactly how to obtain it.	To receive the brochure, a registration form, and a <u>free</u> listing of crafts fairs where you can exhibit, return the enclosed card today.
Show there is no risk.	There is absolutely no obligation. If you decide not to enroll, you may keep the FREE $19.95 crafts fair listing as our gift to you.
	Sincerely yours,

Letter Accompanying a Catalog

Dear _____:

Interest is piqued with an intriguing question.

How many times have you unexpectedly run out of vitamins?

The need is established.

If you're like most of us, you run out frequently. You conscientiously take vitamins because you believe that they help you stay healthy, but because you run out, your vitamin program is interrupted, often for weeks at a time.

The product or service, as a solution to the need, is introduced.

Now, you can eliminate the possibility of running out of vitamins once and for all!

The service is clearly and briefly described.

VitaKing is proud to announce its VitaReminder program. When you purchase more than a month's supply of any vitamin from VitaKing, we'll send you a reminder card two weeks before your supply is depleted. You just call our toll-free number, mention your priority code number (printed on the card), and we rush you your order. It's fast and convenient. And you'll never run out of vitamins again.

The reader is told how to take action.

To enroll in the FREE VitaReminder program, simply mail the enclosed registration card today. You'll notice that the card has a place for you to list the vitamins you currently are using and your remaining supply. Once we receive this information, you'll never have to worry about running out of vitamins again.

The requested action is reinforced.

So, please mail the registration form today. You'll be glad you did.

Sincerely yours,

The benefit of low prices is added in the postscript as a further reason for ordering.

P.S. The VitaReminder program offers you the same low, low pricing you'd expect from VitaKing.

Letter Responding to an Inquiry

Dear _____:

Thank you for your interest in the Sportsman 480 Inflatable Canoe.

Thank the prospect for his or her interest in the product or service.

We have enclosed our new 1988 brochure and price list. You will notice that 15 Sportsman models and many useful accessories are available.

Describe the information you have sent. (Please note that the reader, by inquiring, has already established the need.)

As you know, the Sportsman 480 is the perfect portable canoe. It inflates to 10 feet in length and seats two adults comfortably. When deflated, it easily fits into your car trunk or back seat. The Sportsman weighs only 22 pounds, so you can carry it effortlessly, and it comes complete with an electric pump that plugs into your cigarette lighter. It takes you just two minutes to inflate.

Since the prospect is already interested, do not oversell. Describe the product's most outstanding features. Explain how the prospect will benefit.

When tested by an independent consumer group, the Sportsman 480 was rated the best inflatable canoe available today.

Establish credibility with a testimonial.

You can purchase the Sportsman 480 by calling our 800 number or by visiting one of the fine sporting goods stores listed in the brochure.

Tell the buyer how to order.

Provide an incentive for
ordering now.

If you call now, you can deduct 10 percent from
the already low list price. This special discount
is available for 10 days only, so call today.

Sincerely yours,

A free trial eliminates risk
and is a powerful way to
close.

P.S. We're so sure you'll love your Sportsman
480 that we're offering it to you on a 30-day
free-trial basis. For more details about this no-
risk offer, call the toll-free number today.

Letter Requesting a Donation

Salutation identifies the reader in a positive way.

Dear Animal Lover:

A need is shown.

You can save the giant panda from extinction!

The need is developed further; information is provided that will make the reader's perceived need more powerful.

Did you know that fewer than 1,000 giant pandas are alive today? While this gentle animal was once plentiful, now there are few. And, if nothing is done to help save the panda from extinction, none will remain by the year 2000.

An answer to the problem is suggested.

At Save the Panda, we're taking action now to assure the panda will be here tomorrow. Now you can help.

Show the reader how the contribution will help.

Your contribution goes directly to fund educational and scientific programs that will protect the world panda population and ensure its expansion.

With your support, we can make breakthroughs that will mean the difference between life and death for this animal that has delighted children and adults alike.

Ask for the donation.

I am asking you today to please help Save the Panda. With your gift, we can make great progress toward the survival of the giant panda this year.

Offer a free gift in return for the donation.

I urge you to send in your generous gift. We'll send you FREE a beautiful panda key chain to thank you for your goodwill.

Tell the reader how to send the donation.	Please, fill in the attached pledge card and mail it today.
Closing with a "thank you" shows your expectation of a donation.	Thank you,

CHAPTER 2

LETTERS TO ARRANGE SALES APPOINTMENTS

Most salespeople must make personal sales presentations in order to sell. The more presentations they make to qualified prospects, the more sales they will close. Unfortunately, sales appointments are not easy to arrange. Sales organizations, whether they are one-person businesses or large firms with hundreds of salespeople, constantly need to produce qualified sales leads for their sales personnel.

The most effective medium available for arranging sales appointments is the sales letter. This is because sales letters are inexpensive, easily targeted, and contain all the information necessary to generate interest in your product or service. For your advertising dollar, there is no better way to produce qualified leads for personal sales follow-up.

You can use letters to generate sales appointments in two ways. First, the letter can pave the way for the salesperson to follow up with a telephone call or sales visit. This approach is very effective when the prospect list is both targeted and manageable. For example, if you were selling surgical instruments and had a list of all doctors in the United States, your promotion would probably be ineffective. The list would not be targeted enough, because not all doctors perform surgery. Much of the mailing would be wasted on poor prospects. In addition, the list would be unmanageable, because it would contain too large a population for most sales organizations to handle effectively. However, if the list consisted of surgeons in the states where your company had sales representation, the letter would have an excellent chance of succeeding. Every sugeon in the state would eventually receive a sales call. And, because the surgeons would have read the letter, they would expect the call and be receptive to the presentation.

The second way sales letters generate appointments for sales calls is by asking the prospect to call or return a reply card. This approach is less aggressive but can produce excellent results because every individual who responds is an interested prospect. Also, since there is no follow-up until the prospect requests it, this type of promotion is much less costly than automatically calling or visiting every prospect. While this approach works excellently with well-targeted mailing lists, it is the only approach that makes economic sense with less-targeted lists. A prospect who responds to this type of letter has demonstrated interest in the product or service and should be contacted as soon as possible.

When writing letters to arrange sales appointments, remember that their purpose is to pique the reader's interest. In-depth product descriptions and specifics are best dealt with during the follow-up call. A good rule of thumb would be to present the one or two most important benefits of the product or service in the precall letter. Sell the sizzle, and save the nuts and bolts for later.

Letter Requesting an Appointment—Consumer Product

Dear _____ :

Use a question to identify the need and gain the prospect's interest.

If your home burned down, would you be able to replace the valuable personal and financial papers that you'd lose?

Further explain the problem.

The answer is probably no. Most people keep many one-of-a-kind papers, records, and memorabilia unprotected in their home.

Restate the problem in a way that the prospect can relate to.

Imagine trying to replace photographs, insurance policies, tax returns, deeds, diplomas, marriage licenses, birth certificates, and wills!

Answer the problem with your product or service.

Now your records can be safe from fire. SaveIt Inc. is introducing a new, fireproof file for home use. The SaveIt File keeps all your priceless documents and valuables protected from both fire and water damage.

Describe an additional benefit.

Now you can have the security of a fireproof file at an affordable cost.

Tell the reader what action you wish him or her to take.

To find out how you can own a SaveIt File, return the enclosed reply card or call our toll-free number (1–800–555–5555). Our representative will meet with you and show you how inexpensive owning a fireproof file can be.

Make a special offer.

As a special bonus, we'll present you with a FREE photo inventory of your household possessions when we meet. This record is invaluable in case of a fire loss. And there is no obligation for you to buy anything. Whatever you decide, the photo inventory is our gift to you.

Again ask the prospect to act.

Don't leave yourself unprotected! Send in the reply card or call us today. Remember, you get a FREE photo inventory just for letting us show you the SaveIt File.

Sincerely yours,

Letter Requesting an Appointment—Business Product

Dear _____:

A question that identifies the need captures the reader's interest.

Do misfiled folders often create chaos in your office?

Explain the need. Notice the use of statistics from an independent authority to reinforce the seriousness of the problem.

A recent study by the Association of Office Administrators reports that three out of five offices have serious problems with filing errors. And these mistakes cost companies thousands of dollars a year—in the time it takes employees to locate files and in the customer dissatisfaction caused by misfiling delays.

Answer the need with your product.

Now you can eliminate filing mistakes forever! Find-a-File is a new, color-coded filing system that makes it impossible to place a file in the wrong location. In fact, since Find-a-File makes it so easy to locate the right file, it can actually save you filing time. The secret is in the patented, color-coded, numerically labeled file folder.

Describe the benefits of using the product.

Once you see the system for yourself, you'll see how it can help you:

- Eliminate filing errors
- Save filing time
- Organize your files
- Provide quick visual access

- Simplify your filing procedures
- And more!

Build credibility by mentioning satisfied customers.

Thousands of companies have thrown away their old file folders and have replaced them with modern, efficient Find-a-Files. Shouldn't you, too?

Make a special offer.

To introduce you to Find-a-File, we're offering a FREE, no-obligation survey of your current filing system. We'll review your procedures, give you suggestions on improving your filing system, and show you exactly how much time and money you can save by color-coding with Find-a-File.

Tell the reader when to expect your call.

I will call you next week to see when we can arrange your FREE survey.

Sincerely yours,

Add the benefit of low cost to provide the prospect with an additional reason to want a sales visit.

P.S. You'll be happy to know that Find-a-Files cost no more than the ordinary file folders you're now using!

Letter Requesting an Appointment—Consumer Service

Salutation disarms reader.

Dear Neighbor:

Entice the reader with a powerful benefit that meets a perceived need.

Suppose you could have a magnificent lawn, do no tiresome gardening yourself, and save 20 percent off last year's prices. Would you be interested?

Establish credibility by identifying the community.

Your neighbors in Spring City are enjoying their beautiful lawns now. That's because they use Evergreen Lawn and Garden gardening service. And because so many of your neighbors are using Evergreen, we can save you money!

Explain why the special savings are possible.

Since Evergreen has so many customers in your area, our operation is more efficient. We avoid the time wasted in traveling from one community to another. Because it costs us less to operate in Spring City, we can pass the savings on to you. You actually save 20 percent or more!

Reinforce the special offer and excellent service.

<u>Your neighbors' satisfaction with our service makes this money-saving offer possible!</u>

Explain all aspects of the service.

Evergreen's lawn care service provides all the care you'll need to have a lush, green lawn. We prepare the soil for planting, seed and fertilize, and protect your lawn from fungus and disease. We can do all this or any part of the job. No job is too small at Evergreen.

Naturally, the cost of our service depends on the size of your property.

Restate the offer and tell the reader exactly what action to take.

For your FREE, no-obligation estimate, please call today. I will visit your property and answer any questions you may have.

Sincerely yours,

Use the postscript to reinforce your credibility and to remind the prospect to call.

P.S. If you would like to know the names of your neighbors who use our service, just ask when you call.

Letter Requesting an Appointment—Business Service

Dear _____:

Gain attention by stating a problem with which the prospect can identfiy.

You know how difficult it is to find a reliable supplier of quality printing at a competitive price.

Elaborate on why your service can answer the problem so effectively. If possible, do this in a personal way.

When I received your catalog in the mail this morning, it prompted me to write you.

State the benefits of your service.

You see, if I were to try to find the perfect type of printing job for our equipment, I'd have chosen your catalog. Such an ideal match means we can save you money while meeting your quality and schedule requirements.

Establish credibility.

PennyWise Press has been providing just that service for 20 years. Don't you think it's time we talked?

Invite the reader to learn more about your service.

Find out how working with a small, service-oriented printer like PennyWise Press can be the answer to your printing needs.

Tell the reader that you will call for an appointment.

I will be in your area on Thursday and Friday next week. I will call you in a few days to arrange a meeting convenient to you.

Sincerely yours,

Give the prospect another reason to desire the meeting.

P.S. After reviewing your catalog, I have some exciting ideas to share with you that could cut your costs while increasing your selling space. I look forward to discussing these ideas with you.

Letter Requesting an Appointment—Financial Service

Salutation qualifies reader.	Dear Taxpayer:
Use an attention-getting headline.	TAX ALERT! TAX ALERT! TAX ALERT!
Establish the need.	<u>The new tax law could reduce your discretionary income by 30 percent. That's like losing 30 cents out of every dollar you earn!</u>
Develop the need.	Can you imagine how this substantial decrease in income would affect your lifestyle? It could be devastating.
Hint at a solution to the problem.	Many people are already taking actions to ensure that their income will not be reduced. <u>In fact, by using perfectly legal tax-saving strategies, they may actually increase their after-tax income.</u>
Identify your company and service.	You too can learn how to protect your income with help from Financial Plan, Inc.
State that you can solve the problem.	I would like to show you what must be done <u>now</u> to prepare for the new tax law. I know that once you hear some of my specific recommendations, you'll want to use my low-cost service.
Establish credibility.	I have worked with hundreds of families and can report that every one of them has been able to keep more of its money.

Ask for an appointment. Make it easy for the prospect to accept by offering a free consultation.

I'll call you next week to arrange a convenient time for me to visit you. There is no charge for the visit. It is my way of thanking you for the opportunity to discuss your financial situation with you and show you how I can help you reach your financial goals.

Sincerely yours,

Reinforce your credibility and the promise of your call.

P.S. When I call, I'd be happy to provide you with as many references as you wish.

Letter to a Difficult-to-See Prospect

Dear _____:

Open with an attention-getting question.

Do you believe in the saying, "If at first you don't succeed, try, try again"?

I do, and that's why I'm writing you this letter.

Answer the question in a personal and interesting manner.

I've tried to make an appointment to see you numerous times, but have had no success. Usually, when this happens, I write it off and stop calling. But your situation is different.

You see, I know you need my service.

Show your understanding of the prospect's business and its needs.

Your business, Axon Plumbing and Heating, uses thousands of feet of copper tubing a week. I know this because I supply many of your competitors, and they tell me your business is just like their own.

Describe your product or service and the benefit to the prospect of doing business with you.

Copperco, my company, is the largest supplier of copper tubing in the tristate area. We've saved your competitors money, and we can do the same for you.

Ask for only 15 minutes, and you will probably get a positive answer.

Don't you agree it's worth 15 minutes of your time to see how much money Copperco can save you?

Tell when you plan to call.

I will call you next week to arrange a meeting.

Sincerely yours,

Send information to acquaint the prospect with your company and its services.

P.S. I've enclosed a booklet describing Copperco and the products we distribute.

Letter to a Prospect
Whose Name is Unavailable

Salutation qualifies the reader.	Dear Print Buyer:
A personal comment about the prospect's organization will arouse interest.	Boy, are your telephone personnel terrific!
Explain your difficulty in getting the reader's name.	They were so good at screening my calls that I couldn't even get your name from them. It is a bit awkward writing to a mystery person, but here goes.
Establish the need.	I recently received your course catalog from a friend and realized it would be a perfect printing job for my company. We specialize in newsprint catalogs such as yours.
Name the benefits of using your service.	You'll find our prices highly competitive and our quality and service way above most printers'.
Supply a sample as evidence of your quality.	Enclosed is a job similar to yours. You'll notice the clear printing and sharp reproduction of the halftones. This customer has been a satisfied client for over five years.
Suggest that the prospect call you.	The next step is yours. Why not call me to see how we can fulfill your printing needs?
Use the fact that the prospect's name is unknown to your benefit by using humor to establish rapport.	Just tell me you're "the mystery person" . . . and I'll know exactly who you are.
	I look forward to learning your name.
	Sincerely yours,

CHAPTER 3
FOLLOW-UP LETTERS

Follow-up letters are generally sent after a sales effort has been made but no order has materialized. A well-written follow-up letter will keep the channels of communication open between the salesperson and the customer. And, in many instances, it can motivate the undecided buyer to order. In addition, follow-up letters can be sent after a sale has been lost as a means of staying in contact with the prospect, thereby creating a possibility of future business.

Although many sales departments think follow-up letters are optional, these letters should be sent routinely as part of any sales and customer relations program. Follow-up letters exhibit the professionalism of the sales team. They express the organization's appreciation for the opportunity of making the sales presentation. Moreover, follow-up letters demonstrate the sales team's concern with satisfying the prospect's needs.

Here are some guidelines for writing follow-up letters that produce results:

- Begin by reminding the prospect of the previous sales meeting, letter, telephone call, brochure, or other contact.

- Briefly state what product or service you are offering.

- Repeat the important benefits or special offer.

- Present new information or offers.

- Tell the prospect what you will do next or how he or she can order.

- When appropriate, thank the prospect for his or her interest.

Since you are following up on previous communication, keep the tone of the letter personal and familiar. Try to establish an emotional bond between yourself and the prospect. You can accomplish this by using openings like "You'll remember that last month I offered you . . ." and "I really appreciated your comments about _____ in our July meeting."

Follow-up to a Proposal

Describe the proposal.

Remind the prospect of his or her specific need or interest.

Provide options that will solve the problem and lead to a sale.

Personally state your belief that the product, service, or offer will be of great benefit.

Alert the prospect that you will call to follow up. This shows your diligence and concern.

Dear _____:

Three weeks ago I sent you a quotation on the Danburg 23″ Web Offset Printing Press.

When we met, you expressed an urgent need for this equipment. Although I haven't heard from you, I thought I'd follow up.

In the quotation, I promised delivery within eight weeks. I can still maintain that delivery schedule if you place your order shortly. You can be assured, nevertheless, that whenever you order I will do my best to meet your requirements.

I know, after reviewing your needs and the proposal I sent, the Danburg is the right press for you at the right price.

I will call you next week to see if there is anything I can do to help you make this important decision.

Sincerely yours,

Follow-up to a Meeting

Dear _____:

Thank the prospect for the chance to make the proposal.

I enjoyed our meeting last week and would like to thank you for allowing Dunker and Price to submit a design proposal for your new corporate offices.

Express your enthusiasm for the project.

After seeing the potential of the raw space, I share your excitement and eagerness to get this project under way.

Review what you and the prospect agreed upon at the meeting.

As we discussed, on the 23rd I will send you a preliminary proposal with a rough floor plan. I'll also send you the photos of the Save-All Bank project we discussed. As soon as you send me information on the size and space requirements for your new computer system and have the landlord send me the builder's blueprint, I'll be able to begin work on the proposal.

State how you intend to follow up.

After you have received the proposal and had a chance to review it, I will call you to set up a second meeting. If everything goes as planned, we will be able to finalize the deal by the middle of next month. This would put us right on target for an early-summer completion.

Provide the opportunity for feedback.

If I've forgotten anything or if you have any questions, please call me.

Restate your appreciation.

Again, I appreciate the opportunity to work with you.

Cordially,

Letter Asking for a Second Sale

Dear _____

Capture the customer's attention with a provocative statement.

<u>Four weeks ago you may have made a mistake.</u>

<u>Luckily, there's still time to right it!</u>

Remind the reader of the product's features.

Last month, you purchased a new Turbo 5000 Sports Coupe. You felt the smooth, comfortable ride. You experienced the power upon acceleration. And you appreciated the control in adverse weather conditions.

We waited four weeks before writing you, so you'd really have a chance to learn the true value of the fine automobile you purchased.

Make the follow-up offer.

Now that there's no question in your mind, we'd like to make you the same offer you turned down four weeks ago. You said "NO" to the extended-warranty option last month. Why not reconsider today?

Describe the benefits that the customer will receive.

The extended warranty offers you the same protection you have in your first year of ownership for up to five additional years. Just about everything is covered except normal wear and tear. It saves you money and ensures your car will run as well tomorrow as it does today.

Promote the limited nature of the offer.

This is the last chance you'll have to extend your protection. We will not write you about it again. So act today by returning the enclosed reply card. You'll be glad you did.

Sincerely yours,

Add urgency by restating the limited-time offer.

P.S. Remember, this is your last chance, so take advantage of this important offer now!

Follow-up to a Lost Sale

Dear _____ :

Use the lost sale to establish contact and keep communication open.

Thank you for letting me know that you placed your order for gift-wrapping ribbon with another company.

It is unusual when a customer takes the time to let a salesperson know exactly where he or she stands. I truly appreciate it.

Express your expectation of doing business in the future.

I think that next time Pack-It will be able to meet your packaging needs.

Send information on a product or service that will be of interest to the customer.

I've enclosed Pack-It's new gift-wrapping brochure for your files. You'll notice that we have expanded our line of gift boxes and tissue papers. We now have 23 sizes of boxes and 15 colors of tissue paper, offering you the largest selection available.

Point out a special product, feature, or benefit.

Of special note are the self-adhesive decorative figurines pictured on pages 8 and 9. This is an exclusive new product group. I'm sure you'll think of many creative applications for them.

Tell the customer what action to take.

If you have any questions on the Pack-It line, please call me.

Close by reiterating the hope to do business in the future.

Thanks again for giving me the opportunity to serve you. I hope we can do business in the future.

Sincerely yours,

Follow-up to a Special Offer

Dear _____:

Use the possibility of a lost opportunity to gain attention.

Time is running out!

Restate the special offer.

Last week I offered you a fabulous price on the Universal EasyWrite Word Processor.

Mention the savings benefit. As additional motivation, add the loss of opportunity.

As I explained to you, the manufacturer runs this promotion only once a year. Next week, the same machine will cost you over $100 more. But it's not too late if you act now.

Tell the prospect what must be done to take advantage of the offer.

You can still reserve your word processor at the sale price by calling me or visiting the showroom.

Describe the important features and benefits that previously interested the prospect.

You know from the demonstration that the Universal is the most complete, easy-to-learn word processor on the market today. And because of the special price, it's also the most affordable.

Urge the prospect to act now because of the limited time.

Remember, the price goes up next week, so order today.

Sincerely yours,

Use the postscript to highlight an additional sales point.

P.S. When you call, don't forget to ask about our extended payment plan. It lets you own this great processor for less than $25.00 per month.

Follow-up to a Brochure Mailing

Dear _____:

Remind the prospect of the brochure requested.

Three weeks ago you requested information on the Ultra 2000 Exercise Bicycle, and we were pleased to send you our brochure.

Express your desire to provide further information.

Since we have not heard from you, we thought you might still have some questions about this remarkable advancement in home exercise equipment.

State and answer commonly asked questions.

To help you make the right decision, we thought you might like the answers to the most commonly asked questions about the Ultra 2000.

Use a question to mention a unique feature.

What is the programmable terrain feature?

This is the crux of the exercise system. The bicycle's gears automatically change to simulate up- and downhill terrain according to the level of difficulty you desire.

Explain the benefit the reader will gain.

What do I gain from this feature?

You benefit in two major ways. First, you always get an aerobic workout, because as your endurance increases, you can advance the level of difficulty. Second, by altering the workout from session to session, you eliminate the possibility of boredom.

Answer any concerns that may postpone the decision to buy.

How safe is the system?

Naturally, before beginning any exercise program, you should consult your doctor. The Ultra 2000 is, however, the safest exercise bicycle sold today. As you exercise, your heart rate is automatically monitored, and if you approach overexertion, the machine warns you and shuts itself off.

Restate your desire to assist the prospect.

We hope these questions and answers have been helpful. If you have any further questions, please call our toll-free number, and a customer service representative will be happy to help you.

Sincerely yours,

CHAPTER 4
LETTERS TO CUSTOMERS

Too often, an overall marketing program neglects established customers, as the sales campaign focuses on attracting new customers. But previous buyers offer a special sales opportunity because they know your products and presumably like your service. They are better prospects for a repeat sale than a prospect is for a first-time sale. There is gold in your customer list.

Frequent mailings to customers not only increase sales, but also build loyalty. Your customer is reminded of your business's name, product, and service. Furthermore, your interest in the customer is communicated. Customers like to be recognized, and recognition is a great motivator. A well-conceived and well-written letter to your customers can reestablish their need for your product, awaken new

interest, and inspire purchases. You will find that letters sent to your customers are consistently the most profitable letters you mail.

Sales letters to customers should be less formal and more friendly than letters to prospects. You have already established rapport with the customer, and you should reinforce the relationship. In addition, the customer's *need* has already been established at some level. In these letters, the need, already implicit, does not always have to be defined, as it might be in a "cold" letter. However, you may want to reinforce the need, or try to establish a secondary need. Don't forget that each of these letters is a chance to sell your company, service, or product in some way.

Here are some suggestions for turning your customers into repeat buyers:

- The salutation should use the customer's name whenever possible. If sending individually written, personalized letters is too costly because your mailing list is very large, use "Dear Valued Customer," "Dear Loyal Customer," or "Dear Friend." These salutations can be inexpensively printed on a mass mailing. They recognize the customer as someone special and begin the letter on a positive note.

- Open the letter by acknowledging and thanking the customer for previous business or with a personal or friendly attention-getting statement or question.

- Provide a strong offer or a new reason for the customer to buy.

- When your relationship with the customer is friendly and the letter is positive, end your letter with a friendly, informal closing such as "Cordially yours."

- Let the customer know that you understand he or she expects and deserves special treatment.

Note: Please see the next chapter, "Customer Service Letters," for more letters to customers.

Letter Welcoming a New Client

Dear _____:

Extend a personal welcome.

As President of Davidson and Sloan Advertising, I would like to personally welcome you as a new client.

Express your enthusiasm for the new business arrangement.

Nancy Greene, your account executive, has told me about your company, and we are all excited about helping you achieve your marketing goals.

Use this opportunity to positively reinforce your company.

I always enjoy welcoming new clients because it gives me the opportunity to explain the D&S philosophy. It is because of this philosophy that we have been so successful in helping our clients meet and exceed their advertising objectives.

We at D&S believe in what we call "110 percent service." One hundred percent is not good enough. This means that on every project we give you more than you expect, more than you pay for. By consistently going the extra mile, we create advertising that works. This is how we earn your confidence and continued business.

Express your desire to build a personal relationship.

I look forward to personally meeting you in the near future.

Sincerely yours,

Letter Introducing a New Product

Dear _____:

Identify the new need and introduce a new product that will solve the problem.

You can drastically cut your winter heating bills with Webco Super-Insulated Storm Doors!

Reestablish your relationship with the customer. Use the customer's past satisfaction to help sell the new product.

As an owner of Webco Super-Insulated Storm Windows, you already are seeing significant heating-fuel savings. Now you can increase those savings with Webco Storm Doors.

Make an exclusive offer to customers.

We are telling our customers about these exciting new products before anyone else. This way you can schedule your door's installation before the rush and be sure to save energy dollars this winter.

Promise useful information along with product data.

We've reserved a copy of our information brochure, Webco Storm Doors—Your Fuel Saver, for you. It provides you with many tips on "winterizing" your home along with specifications, styles, and prices of Webco Super-Insulated Storm Doors.

Tell the customer to get the information.

For your FREE copy, call us today or return the enclosed postcard.

Suggest a benefit for acting immediately.

By acting now, you'll be assured a warm, energy-efficient winter.

Sincerely yours,

Add a final product benefit.

P.S. Like our storm windows, our storm doors cost at least 20 percent less than any other high-quality storm door available!

Letter Introducing a New Service

Dear _____:

Establish rapport by congratulating the customer for his or her wise use of your service.

Last year you graduated from the Baker Evans Sales Leadership Course, and we'd like to congratulate you again on your personal achievement.

Enhance interest with the promise of an important benefit.

We know you'd like to learn about an exciting development at Baker Evans that can help you excel in possibly the most difficult area of sales management . . . recruiting salespeople who will succeed.

Announce the new service.

We would like to introduce the new Baker Evans Sales Placement Service.

Describe the service and the benefits the customer will derive.

This unique placement service will find you sales trainees with the proper attitudes and motivation for success in sales. And this service costs you a fraction of what traditional placement services cost.

Create credibility by explaining how you can deliver your promise.

"How," you may ask, "can Baker Evans do this?" The answer is simple. Every applicant is a graduate of the Baker Evans Introductory Sales Course. And we make sure they have the right stuff. Since this service helps us sell our course and doesn't really cost us much to implement, we pass the savings on to you.

Review the benefits of the service.

You save time and money. You no longer have to advertise for new salespeople or use expensive placement services. And, since all applicants are screened and trained by us, you never waste time interviewing unqualified people.

Let the customer know that you will follow up soon.

We will call you in a few days to discuss this innovative approach to your sales personnel needs.

Use a friendly closing.

Cordially yours,

Letter Introducing a New Salesperson

Dear _____:

Start with an interesting statement.

I have some <u>good news</u> for you . . . and some <u>more good news!</u>

Positively announce that the previous salesperson has moved on.

John Clark has been your account executive for over five years. I know you will be very happy for John when you hear his good news. John has been appointed Southwest Regional Manager for his outstanding achievements at Forward Computer Technologies.

Reassure the customer that the excellent service will not change.

This means that John will no longer service your account. But it does not mean that your excellent working relationship with Forward will be jeopardized.

Include the old salesperson in the announcement of the new employee. Be extremely positive and enthusiastic about the replacement.

John and I are pleased to announce some more good news—the appointment of Martha Crain as your new account executive. Martha has been an important member of our sales team for three years, and for the last six months she has been trained by John. Martha's strong computer background, superior product knowledge, and painstaking attention to detail make her a first-rate account executive.

Show your personal interest in the customer's welfare during this change.

Because I want this transition to be extremely smooth, I would like to introduce Martha to you. I will call to arrange an appointment at your convenience.

Sincerely yours,

Letter Announcing a Brochure or Catalog

The salutation and opening question build a relationship between the writer and the reader.

Dear Worldwide Customer:

Would you do me a personal favor?

A provocative statement is used to pique the reader's interest.

I'm the advertising manager at Worldwide Sea Shells, and my job is at stake!

And as a long-standing customer of Worldwide Sea Shells, you are the only one who can help.

Interest is maintained with a personal narrative.

You see, I was really tired of our old black-and-white catalog. It didn't show off the vibrant colors and intricate natural designs of the shells we offer.

So I convinced my boss to spend a fortune redoing this entire catalog in full color. It had better increase sales, or I'm in a lot of trouble.

Well, here it is, and even my boss says it looks great.

Ask for the action desired. Promise a benefit.

The favor? Spend a few moments reviewing each page. You'll see some of the most extraordinary sea shells we've ever presented.

Once you've looked through the catalog, you'll find ordering irresistible. You'll love what you buy, and my boss will love me.

Urge the reader to act immediately.

Please review the catalog now! The sooner you do, the sooner you'll see these remarkable natural creations, and the sooner my job will be secure.

Sincerely yours,

Refer to a specific page to get the reader involved in the catalog or brochure.

P.S. See page 14 for three rare shells just discovered in the South Pacific and offered for the first time.

Letter Announcing a Special Sale

The salutation makes the customer feel appreciated.

Dear Valued Customer:

Announce the sale and invite the customer.

Once a year we invite our best customers to our gala preview open house . . . and since you're one of our best customers, you're invited!

Recognize the customer with a special privilege.

Our biggest sale of the year takes place next Thursday. But before it is open to the public, we give our favorite customers the opportunity to join us the night before for wine, cheese, and SAVINGS. You get to choose the best bargains first, with no crowds or hassles.

Provide the details of the sale.

So please accept our invitation and join us on Wednesday evening. The festivities begin at 6:30 and last until 10:00.

Close warmly.

Cordially yours,

Entice the reader to attend with the promise of new merchandise and sale prices.

P.S. We just received over 200 magnificent crystal gift items imported from Italy. This fine stemware will be on sale Wednesday night only, so come early!

Letter to Build Store Traffic

Salutation reminds the reader of the established relationship.	Dear Loyal Smith's Customer:
Thank the customer for previous business.	THANK YOU, THANK YOU, THANK YOU. Your patronage of Smith's last year helped make it the most successful in our 60 years here in Newtown. Without you, we couldn't have done it!
Include the customer in a special celebration or offer.	To show our appreciation, we are instituting what we call "The Great Event Days and Sale" here at Smith's. And you're invited!
Enthusiastically promote the sale.	We'll have some really exciting things "'in store" for you every Wednesday for the next 10 weeks.
Detail the event or offer.	It all starts next Wednesday, the 23rd, at 12:00 at the atrium level. • You'll see a Spring Fashion Show. • You'll learn how to prepare an elegant brunch. • You'll meet the author of *Home Businesses You Can Start for Under $1,000.* • Plus we'll have many surprises you won't want to miss.
Add the benefit of reduced prices.	Also, hundreds of items will be placed on sale for Wednesday and Wednesday only!

Remind the customer to save the date.	So please, mark your calendar for next Wednesday and each Wednesday thereafter for a special afternoon at Smith's. You won't be disappointed.
	Sincerely yours,
Close with a personal expression of your appreciation.	P.S. As owner of Smith's, I am looking forward to Wednesday, when I can personally thank you for shopping at Smith's.

Letter to Renew a Subscription

The salutation qualifies the reader.

Dear Subscriber:

Reinforce the need for the product.

Thank goodness, there's still time to renew your subscription to *Home Design* magazine without missing an issue.

Mention memorable features from previous issues to motivate the reader to renew.

This year, *Home Design* presented dozens of provocative ideas that have caused a sensation in the design world. You read about:

- Turning Your Mate On with Sexy Lighting
- Your Bathroom . . . Your Spa
- Color Schemes That Enhance Sleep
- Seating Arrangements That Promote Good Conversation

We promise that every issue of *Home Design* to come will be just as stimulating.

Introduce a special offer.

Don't miss one great article. Renew your subscription now and take advantage of some truly remarkable savings.

Explain the discount. Get the subscriber involved by providing choices.

Choose the offer you like best or write your own deal by checking the appropriate box below.

☐ 1-Year Subscription . . . Save 33%

☐ 2-Year Subscription . . . Save 42%

☐ 3-Year Subscription . . . Save 52%

☐ __-Year Subscription . . . Save 60% (Write your own deal—as many years as you wish over three years.)

Make responding easy.	Don't send any money. Just return the subscription form in the postage-paid envelope. You will be billed later.
Reinforce the benefit of uninterrupted service.	Renew today! We'll rush your next issue of *Home Design* to you. You won't miss any hot trends in home decoration.
	Sincerely yours,
Provide an additional reason for ordering.	P.S. Be sure to see our new monthly feature, *Decorating on a Shoestring*, debuting in the next fact-filled issue!

Letter to an Inactive Account

Dear _____:

Open with an attention-getting headline.

I could hardly believe it . . .

Express your surprise at losing the customer's business.

And so I checked twice, but it's true. We haven't received an order for silk flowers from you in almost a year.

Offer to go out of the way to regain the customer's trust.

Whenever I learn that a good customer like you has stopped calling on us, I get very worried. Losing a good customer is like losing a good friend. Was it something we did? If so, we'd like to make it up to you.

Describe a new product or service to interest the former customer.

Our new fall line has just arrived. It is the most exciting, most colorful, and possibly the most creative silk flower line ever introduced. I know you won't want to miss it.

Provide an incentive for the customer to buy again.

I want to offer you a special 20 percent discount on your next order. It's my way of telling you how much we value your business.

Warmly suggest that the customer visit or call you.

I invite you to visit our showroom and see the new line for yourself. Whether you visit us or order through our catalog, the 20 percent discount is yours.

Won't you call or come in soon?

Sincerely yours,

Letter to a Long-Term Inactive Account

After other attempts have failed at reaching the client, this strong approach may be used as a last chance effort.

A mild threat will usually get this "lost" customer to at least read the letter.

Express your dismay in a personal manner.

Restate the benefits that the customer appreciated when last served.

Make a sincere appeal to correct the situation.

Dear _____:

THIS IS THE LAST LETTER YOU WILL RECEIVE FROM US!

If you do not answer, we will assume that you no longer have any need for Redco PolyExtrusions. And we will not bother you again.

But we must express our surprise and disappointment. We're losing a loyal and valued customer.

Last year you purchased extrusions from us every month. You praised the high quality and low price of our products. Now it has been over a year since your last order.

Before giving up, we decided to write you this last letter. Please tell us what we can do to win back your business. Perhaps we failed you in some manner. If we have, please let us know how.

We look forward to hearing from you.

Sincerely yours,

Letter Asking a Previous Donor for a Gift

<table>
<tr><td>

Salutation establishes a relationship.

Open with a personal, complimentary statement.

Praise the donor for last year's help.

Describe the charity's mission.

Ask for the donor's assistance. Emphasize its importance. Make the request as personal as possible. The reader should feel that the program depends on his or her generosity.

</td><td>

Dear Friend,

<u>Good people like you are hard to find.</u>

Your generous donation last year has helped Jeff Stone (see enclosed photograph), and children like him, face their last days peacefully.

As you know, the Wish Upon A Star Foundation fulfills the fantasies and wishes of children with catastrophic diseases. It gives these children something to look forward to and memories to cherish for their remaining days.

Last year, your contribution and those of compassionate individuals like you helped realize the dreams of over 150 deserving children.

We ask for your generosity again. Our program depends on your contribution. This year, we need as much help as you can give, since there are more children in the program than ever before.

</td></tr>
</table>

Tell the reader what action to take.

Help us make each child's wish come true. Please enclose your donation in the envelope provided and send it to us today.

Close by assuming the donor will contribute.

Thank you for your continued goodwill.

Sincerely yours,

Letter Asking for a Referral

Dear _____:

Thank the customer for previous patronage. Add a friendly, personal word.

I have just received your order, the third this year, and want to thank you for it. We've been doing business for eight years now, and I consider you one of my most valued customers.

Ask for the referral.

May I ask you a favor? As a Hatfield customer, you have learned that Hatfield Ball Bearings are the finest manufactured in the United States. You have found our prices to be very competitive and our service to be outstanding. Being a leader in your industry, you probably know and are friendly with many companies that could use our products. A referral coming from you would carry a lot of weight.

Provide the customer with the option of accepting or declining the request.

Some people make it a matter of policy not to offer referrals, and if you feel this way, we understand. If, however, you feel comfortable providing us with a referral, it would be greatly appreciated.

Tell the customer when you will call, and express your desire for a continued business relationship.

I will give you a call next week to see what you have decided. Whatever your decision, I look forward to serving you in the future.

Use a friendly closing.

Cordially yours,

CHAPTER 5

CUSTOMER SERVICE LETTERS

A company's single most important asset is its customers. And to keep customers, a company must provide good service. More customers are lost because of poor, unresponsive service than because of keen competition.

An essential part of a customer service program is the customer service letter. Successful customer service replies are *responsive, sympathetic,* and *personal.*

A *responsive* customer service letter is one that immediately answers the customer's questions and addresses the customer's problems. If an answer or solution is not quickly available, the customer is told exactly when to expect additional information. *Speed is essential.* Whenever possible, a customer service letter should be written the day the problem is discovered. A fast response communicates the company's respect and concern for the customer. It tells the customer that he or she is dealing with a professional organization.

A *sympathetic* response to a customer's problem can be more effective than a solution to the problem. Being sympathetic means putting yourself in the customer's position and seeing the problem from his or her perspective. When a customer tells you of a problem, reply that you understand how upset he or she is and that the anger is justified. Explain that you'd feel the same way in this situation. This instantly disarms the customer. You take the wind out of his or her sails and more often than not win his or her goodwill and loyalty. Many a savvy marketing executive has said, "The customer is always right." A wise addendum would be, "A customer with a problem is even *more* right."

When people have been wronged, they want an apology. They do not want to hear excuses. *Therefore, apologize for an error if you are in the wrong, and also apologize for an error when you are in the right.* Go out of your way to make amends. Provide a toll-free number, free return shipping, postage-paid reply envelope, gift certificate, or some other device to demonstrate your sympathy for the customer's situation. Whatever it costs will be paid back quickly in customer loyalty.

Make your letter *personal.* Nothing irks an already angry customer more than receiving a form letter. Use your name and suggest the customer call you if the problem is not resolved satisfactorily. Needless to say, the letter should be individually typed with the customer's name in the salutation.

By making sure that your customer service letters are *responsive, sympathetic,* and *personal,* you'll solve problems quickly and turn customer dissatisfaction into confidence.

Complaint Resolution Letter— Customer Is Right

Dear _____:

Disarm the customer by agreeing with the complaint.

I have reviewed the situation you described in your letter of July 23, and I agree with you completely.

Describe the error.

A mistake was made when your order was not shipped because of credit problems. There is no question that you have *never* been a credit risk and, in fact, have an excellent credit history with our company.

Apologize for the mistake. Assure the customer that it will not happen again.

I apologize for the error and have made sure the sales and accounting departments realize that you can do business with us on open account. Your credit line has been increased to $50,000. That's $15,000 more than your previous limit.

Explain how the error will be corrected. When possible, offer the customer something extra to make amends.

I have also instructed our warehouse to immediately release your order of July 7 for shipment. As a way of showing how sorry we are for the error, we will pay the freight charges on that order.

Restate your apology.

Again, please accept my apologies. And let me know if there is anything further I can do. I look forward to serving you in the future.

Sincerely yours,

Complaint Resolution Letter— Customer Is Wrong

Dear _____:

Thank the customer for writing and describe the problem.

Thank you for your letter of January 21, in which you describe our credit department's denial of credit on your recent order as "unfair."

State your reason for declining the credit request.

I want you to know that we are very careful to be as fair as possible when making a decision on whether or not to grant credit. The information we received from the references you supplied did not sufficiently answer our credit questions.

Provide the customer with an opportunity to send more information.

If you can provide further information or additional references, we would be happy to review our decision.

Tell the customer what to do.

Until then, you can place your orders on a cash-on-delivery basis.

Express your hope for continued business.

We look forward to serving you.

Sincerely yours,

Complaint Stopgap Letter

NOTE: This is a response to a problem when all information is not yet available.

Acknowledge the complaint and offer your apology.

Describe the situation as you see it.

State your concern for the customer, and specify when you intend to solve the problem.

Apologize again.

Dear _____:

Your letter of November 17 has just come to my attention. I am very sorry to hear that you are dissatisfied with the service you received.

As I understand the situation, you have repeatedly called our sales department regarding an order you placed on September 15. The order is three weeks late, and no one has been able to provide you with a definite delivery date. In addition, many of your phone calls have not been returned.

There is no excuse for treating any customer in such a manner, especially a long-standing, valued customer like you. I will look into the matter personally, and will call you on Friday morning with a firm delivery date.

Again, I apologize, and thank you for bringing this situation to my attention.

Sincerely yours,

Apology for an Employee's Rudeness

Open by thanking the customer for bringing the problem to your attention. Show your honest concern for the customer.

Tell what action you have taken to solve the problem.

State that the incident is unusual and that your staff is trained to deal with customers in a professional manner.

Apologize again and emphasize the importance you place on customer satisfaction.

Dear _____:

Thank you for relating the unfortunate incident last week in which a telephone representative was discourteous to you. I want to offer my personal apology and my promise that such inappropriate behavior will not occur again.

I have spoken with the employee about proper conduct and have taken action to see that his attitude will change. I believe he realizes the gravity of his error.

Our telephone representatives know the value of customers like you and are trained to handle your inquiries and problems efficiently and professionally. Unfortunately, mistakes do happen.

Please accept my apology. Your satisfaction and continued goodwill are our most important concern.

Sincerely yours,

Apology for a Product Defect

Dear _____:

Apologize for the problem. Show that you sympathize with the customer and intend to solve the problem immediately.

Thank you for notifying us about the malfunction of your dishwasher. We understand how disturbing it is to purchase a new product and have problems with it. We promise to have your dishwasher working perfectly.

State that the incident is unusual.

The dishwasher you purchased is one of the finest made, and problems with it are very unusual.

Explain exactly how and when the problem will be solved.

Our service department is the best in the business and is about to contact you as this letter is being written. They will arrange a repair time convenient to you. Naturally, your dishwasher is under full warranty, and there will be no charge for parts or labor.

Apologize again and stress the value you put on excellent customer service.

Please accept our apology for the inconvenience you have suffered. Our business depends on satisfied customers, and we will do everything in our power to make you happy.

Sincerely yours,

Apology for a Problem Outside Your Responsibility

Dear _____:

Apologize for the problem even though it was not your responsibility.

I was very sorry to hear about the delivery problems you encountered last Tuesday and Wednesday. I can think of nothing more frustrating than waiting home for a promised delivery that never arrives.

Explain why the responsibility is not yours.

As you know, the delivery company was not our own, but one you hired in order to arrange an earlier delivery. As much as we sympathize with you, we cannot take responsibility for their lack of professionalism.

Your furniture was at our warehouse and ready for pickup Tuesday morning. The delivery truck did not arrive until Thursday morning.

Take some action to show that you support the customer.

We intend to write the delivery company a letter disapproving of their treatment of you. You can be assured that we will never use their delivery services.

Close by apologizing again.

Again, we are sorry about the unfortunate incident.

Sincerely yours,

Out-of-Stock Letter

Dear _____:

Thank the customer for the order and inform him or her of the depletion of stock.

Thank you for your order for Elite Christmas Ornament Assortment sets. Unfortunately, due to its popularity, we are temporarily out of stock on that item.

Tell the customer when to expect the order. Provide an alternative to waiting.

We are expecting a new shipment within two weeks. You can wait for that shipment, or you can order the Deluxe Assortment, which is in stock. The Deluxe Assortment is the same as the Elite, except that it does not contain the five-pointed star ornament.

Let the customer know exactly what you will do and what is expected of him or her.

We will hold a supply of the Deluxe Assortment for you and give you an additional 10 percent off on the substitution. Please let us know if you want us to ship it or if you'd rather wait for the Elite Assortment to arrive.

Apologize and suggest a way of avoiding the situation in the future.

We apologize for the inconvenience that you have suffered. To prevent this back-order situation from occurring again, we will stock a much larger supply of the Elite Assortment in the future.

Thank the customer again for the order.

Again, thank you for the order. We will wait to hear from you with instructions on how to proceed.

Cordially yours,

Minimum Order Letter

Acknowledge the order and thank the customer.

Diplomatically inform the customer of the minimum order size.

Explain what benefit the customer receives because of the minimum.

Provide an opportunity for the customer to increase the size of the order.

Express your thanks.

Note: An alternative approach is to fulfill the below-minimum order as a courtesy while notifying the customer of the future minimum order requirement.

Dear _____:

Thank you for your order of October 20 for 10 reams of number A5364 photocopy paper.

As a new customer, you may be unaware that our minimum order is $200. Your order does not reach that minimum.

To keep our photocopy supply prices as low as they are, we cannot handle orders at less than our minimum. You buy at a discount because we sell in volume.

We have enclosed our complete price list of photocopy supplies and office stationery. I hope you can find some additional items you need that will bring your order to $200.

Thank you again for your interest.

Sincerely yours,

Notice of Price Increase

Salutation makes customer feel important.

Show your concern over the price increase by stating your historical reluctance to raise prices.

Provide the customer with advance notice so he or she can make appropriate plans.

If the increase is small, state this as a benefit.

Sell your pricing if it is still competitive.

Assure the customer of your commitment to holding prices down in the future.

Dear Valued Customer:

The last thing I want to write you about is a price increase. As you know, we have increased prices only three times in the last 10 years. But because of steady increases in the cost of the materials we use, we can no longer hold prices.

We hope that by writing you this letter well in advance of the increase, you'll have time to stock up on our products at the old prices.

I'm sure you'll be pleased to learn that we are increasing prices only 3 percent, and only on the items indicated on the attached list. All other prices will remain as before.

Even with the increase, you'll find our prices are still below those of the competition.

Thank you again for your patronage and understanding. I will do my best to maintain this price level for as long as possible.

Cordially yours,

Notice of Price Decrease

Address customer warmly.	Dear Valued Customer:
Enthusiastically inform the customer of the price decrease.	I take great pleasure in writing you this letter to announce a price decrease.
	<u>Yes, you read it correctly. We are decreasing prices!</u>
Thank the customer for the continued business.	And my thanks go to you for making this possible. Because of our customers' increased business, we've been able to step up production and thereby realize substantial cost savings. I am happy to pass these savings on to you.
Explain the new price structure.	Beginning the first of July, all glassware will be reduced 10 percent, and all crystal 5 percent. We will maintain this price decrease for three months, until the first of October.
Urge the customer to act while the prices are low.	Remember, the new prices are in effect for a limited time, so place your order today!
	Sincerely yours,

Letter Granting Permission to Return Merchandise

Dear _____:

Acknowledge the problem.

We are sorry to learn that your recently purchased carving knives have become discolored.

Show how you will solve the problem. Make it easy for the customer to return the merchandise.

The best way to correct this problem is for us to replace the knives with a new set. We've enclosed a preaddressed shipping container for your convenience. Just mail the knives back to us, and we will rush you your new knives, along with a certificate entitling you to $5 off your next purchase from Cutlery Corner. It's our way of apologizing for the trouble we've caused you.

Reassure the customer of the quality of the replacement.

After investigating the problem you described, we found that one shipment of knives from the manufacturer was defective. You can be assured that the new knives we send you will be perfect.

Personally guarantee the customer's satisfaction.

At Cutlery Corner, your satisfaction is our most important concern. We are sure you'll be very pleased with your knives, but if there should be any problem, please contact me personally.

Close on a positive note.

We look forward to serving you again in the near future.

Sincerely yours,

Letter Refusing a Return of Merchandise

Dear _____:

Sympathize with the customer's problem.

We are very sorry to learn that the stereo system you purchased from us is not working properly.

Explain the company policy.

As you'll remember, you purchased the stereo "on sale" at a significant discount. At the time of sale, it was explained to you that the sale would be final and that our normal return policy would not be in effect. You were also urged to inspect the stereo immediately at home and to call us if a problem existed. It has been three months since your purchase.

I have enclosed a copy of the sales receipt showing the final sales terms and your signature.

Firmly and clearly decline acceptance of the return.

I'm sure you can understand that under those terms of sale, we cannot accept the return of your stereo.

Provide information to help the customer as a token of goodwill.

You can have the stereo repaired at our service center or at any authorized service company. If you choose our service department, we will be pleased to extend you a 25 percent discount. I have included a list of authorized service companies in your area.

Sincerely yours,

Volume Discount Letter

Dear _____:

Thank the customer for the order.

Thank you for your order of May 8 for 15 correctable typewriter cassettes.

Explain the volume discount.

Because you are ordering 15 cassettes, you are entitled to a 5 percent discount. You may not be aware, however, that if you order 4 more cassettes, to make your order total 19, you'll receive a 10 percent discount.

Ask the customer to increase the order and to respond quickly.

Please call us to let us know whether to increase the quantity or not, so we can rush your order to you. We will not ship until we hear from you.

Provide the customer with the current volume discount schedule.

For your future reference, here's our quantity discount schedule.

Quantity	Volume Discount
1–5	none
6–18	5%
19–47	10%
48–95	15%
96–149	20%
150 & over	25%

For orders over 500 units, please call for a quotation.

Say thanks again.

Thank you again for your order.

Sincerely yours,

Letter Concerning Service No Longer Offered

Dear _____:

Describe your business and focus on the benefits that have attracted the customer in the past.

As you know, Patent Research Inc. provides research and consultation on patent registration at low-cost, hourly rates. We've been successful because we help you realize savings while quickly finding you the information you require.

Explain the nature of the service that is to be changed.

Because our clients need answers fast, we correspond using overnight mail services. Up to now, we've been able to absorb these costs.

Inform the reader as to exactly what you will do.

The cost of overnight mail has been rising, as has the frequency with which we've been using it in our clients' behalf. So that we can keep our hourly rates low, we will begin charging our clients for the overnight mail we use for their assignments. These costs will be billed separately and will not be marked up.

Emphasize that after the change the customer will still get excellent service.

This new policy will allow us to maintain our low hourly rates at their present level. And, if you do not require overnight delivery, you will not have to pay for it.

Thank the customer for accepting the change.

Thank you for your understanding in this matter.

Sincerely yours,

Assure the customer that when he or she must pay for the service, it will be at the lowest possible rate.

P.S. When we do use overnight delivery services for you, we use the least expensive carriers available.

Vacation Shutdown Letter

Dear _____ :

Inform the customer, well in advance, of the dates of the shutdown.

Atlas Polybags will shut down for its yearly two-week vacation from August 2 to August 16. No business will be conducted during this period.

Use this opportunity to say something positive about your company.

As you know, this has been a very busy year at Atlas. We have expanded our manufacturing facilities by 20 percent, increased our staff, and cut the time between receipt of order and shipment by an average of two days.

These improvements mean that the good service we've provided for you for over 20 years will be even better.

Let the customer know when business will resume.

After such an ambitious year, the two-week vacation is just what the doctor ordered. We'll be back on August 17, well rested, enthusiastic, and ready to serve you.

Thank the customer for his or her patronage.

Thank you for helping us make this such an exciting time at Atlas.

Cordially yours,

Provide instructions in case of an emergency.

P.S. If you have an emergency and must speak to us during the vacation period, please call this special number: _____ . Also, you might consider placing your orders in advance of the vacation shutdown.

CHAPTER 6

GOODWILL LETTERS

Goodwill letters are letters sent to customers, prospects, business associates, and friends in order to express your interest and concern for their well-being. While goodwill letters are not considered sales letters, they can help cement established sales relationships and improve tenuous ones.

Some sales organizations include sales messages in their goodwill letters. This should generally be avoided, as it raises questions about the motivation of the letter. Your genuine interest in the other person is all you should wish to convey. That interest will be long remembered and appreciated.

Here are some pointers to consider when writing goodwill letters:

- Goodwill letters should be brief and to the point.

- Goodwill letters should be personal. Avoid stilted, formal language.

- Goodwill letters should be sincere. Express your honest feelings.

- Goodwill letters should be timely. They must be sent as close to the event as possible.

- Goodwill letters should be factual. Do not make any assumptions about circumstances or people. Stick to what you know to be true.

- Goodwill letters should be appropriate to your relationship with the individual. Don't make the error of assuming your relationship is friendlier or closer than it really is.

Thank You for an Order or Purchase

Dear _____:

Acknowledge the order or purchase and welcome the new customer.

Thank you for ordering the <u>Success Today</u> audio cassette program. I would personally like to welcome you as a new customer.

Praise the customer for the decision to buy.

You have taken a major step toward realizing your dreams. It's clear that you've made a commitment to career success.

Let the customer know that using the product will meet his or her expectations.

You'll find listening to the <u>Success Today</u> program an exciting and rewarding experience. Once you have completed the course and begin to use the principles in your day-to-day life, you will see your career take off.

Promise to send additional information to the new customer. (Use the information to be sent as an opportunity to sell other products.)

In addition, as a new customer, you'll be receiving our complimentary <u>Success</u> newsletter. It's our way of saying thanks to new customers every month. The newsletter contains many intriguing ideas and tips to help you accomplish your goals. In addition, each issue will feature information on other motivational audio cassette programs from Success Unlimited.

Close by thanking the customer again.

Thank you again for your order.

Sincerely yours,

Thank You for a Large Order or Big Purchase

Show your enthusiasm and express thanks for the large order or purchase.

Give the status of the order.

Close by thanking the customer again. Show your expectation for future business.

Dear _____:

Two-hundred and fifty lobster pots! That's the largest order we've received from a retailer for this item, and I want to thank you for it.

Your order will be sent in two shipments. I will have 100 pots on the way to you by the end of the week, and the remainder of the order will be shipped next week.

Thank you again for such a large order. I look forward to your continued success with our lobster pots.

Cordially yours,

P.S. This spring we are introducing a deluxe lobster pot that also steams clams. I'll send you a sample as soon as it is available.

Thank You for Repeat Business

Dear _____:

Acknowledge the order and extend your thanks.

We have received your order of September 22 for 25,000 #10 envelopes and would like to thank you.

Make a personal comment about doing business with the customer.

Your order reminded me that we have been doing business for quite some time. After checking, I was really surprised to learn that it has been over four years since your first order.

Express your appreciation in a sincere manner.

Your business has helped us grow, and we appreciate it very much. Moreover, it is rare to find people who conduct business in such a professional and agreeable manner as you.

Always close by thanking the customer again.

Thank you again for your order.

Sincerely yours,

Thank You for Courtesies Shown

Show appreciation for the hospitality.

Mention an enjoyable incident or experience while on the visit.

Give thanks to others who were of assistance.

Offer to reciprocate and show your expectation of continuing relationship.

Use a warm and friendly closing.

Note: This letter is written in a very personal manner. The level of familiarity can differ depending upon the nature of the relationship.

Dear _____:

I would like to thank you for the kindness you showed me on my recent sales trip. Your thoughtfulness made my visit truly memorable.

I really enjoyed the tour of your manufacturing facility—it is an impressive operation. Just as enjoyable was the walk through historic Old Northwich and that great dinner at Greenwoods.

Please express my appreciation to Linda, Tony, and Robert. Their personal warmth made me feel right at home.

We discussed your visiting us in the near future. I look forward to your being my guest. I know you'll enjoy Carefree Beach and its amenities.

Again, thank you for your kindness.

Cordially yours,

Thank You for a Testimonial (Unsolicited)

Dear _____:

Thank the customer for the testimonial.

I would like to thank you for the testimonial I just received. Your praise of our dealership and its service department is most gratifying.

Offer warm and personal praise to the testimonial giver.

It is unusual for someone to take the time to express his or her satisfaction with a product or service. It's people like you who make our special effort worthwhile.

Take the opportunity to reinforce the benefit of the product or service.

I am very pleased that you like your new Turbo Coupe as much as you do. When I sold it to you, I really believed it was the ideal car for your needs. I hope it gives you many years of enjoyment.

Give thanks again in as personal a way as possible.

Thank you again for the testimonial. I'm proud to know I've been of service.

Close informally.

Cordially yours,

Thank You for a Testimonial (Solicited)

Dear _____ :

Thank the customer for responding to your request.

I would like to thank you for sending the enthusiastic testimonial letter that I just received. Your kind response to my request for comments about our products is greatly appreciated.

Make a personal comment about the testimonial.

I am pleased to have served you for 11 years and am glad that you have recommended our products to many of your friends.

Use the opportunity to reinforce the positive relationship.

Loyal customers like you are hard to find. I promise to do everything in my power to maintain the high standards of quality and service you have learned to expect from us.

Thank the customer again.

Again, thank you so much for the glowing testimonial.

Sincerely yours,

Thank You for a Referral

Thank the individual for making a referral.

Give the status of the referral.

State your appreciation in a personal way.

Thank the individual again.

Use a friendly closing.

Dear _____:

Thank you for suggesting to Jack Davis that he call me regarding his software needs.

I met with Jack on Tuesday and enjoyed talking with him. I am sure that he and I will be doing business in the near future.

Jack mentioned how enthusiastic and complimentary you were in giving him my name. I truly appreciate your confidence in my abilities.

Thank you again for thinking of me.

Cordially yours,

Best Wishes on a Promotion

Express your happiness for the individual. Make a personal comment.

Express your expectation of a continued business relationship.

Dear _____:

Let me offer my sincere congratulations on your recent promotion. From the day I met you, I knew you were destined for great things.

I'm so pleased that your ability has been recognized and rewarded. You must be very gratified with your accomplishment.

I do hope that in your new position we can continue to work together.

Cordially yours,

Best Wishes on a
New Appointment

Dear _____:

Express your congratulations and pleasure at learning of the appointment.

I was so happy to learn that you had been appointed chairperson of the Musical Instrument Manufacturers Association's annual meeting and convention. You have always been highly dedicated and hardworking, and certainly deserve this honor.

Volunteer your support.

I understand the magnitude of this project and want to offer my assistance whenever you need it.

Make a personal comment.

I know from our many years of working together that you will make this year's convention the most successful we've ever held.

End by repeating the congratulations.

Congratulations again!

Use a friendly closing.

Cordially yours,

Best Wishes on a Business Achievement

Dear _____ :

Offer your congratulations.

Congratulations!

Acknowledge the business achievement.

Just last week I read about the new aerosol dispenser you introduced at the International Packaging Show. You must be very proud of your accomplishment.

Express your admiration.

It seems that every year you are responsible for many of the innovations in our industry. Your ability to remain at the forefront of creative development amazes me.

Restate your congratulations.

Again, congratulations on your new product. I look forward to offering you my compliments in person at the association meeting next month.

Use a friendly closing.

Cordially yours,

Best Wishes on a
Business Anniversary

Dear _____:

Acknowledge the occasion and offer your congratulations.

I was very pleased to hear that this month marks the 15th anniversary of Janice Fashions. I'd like to extend my sincere congratulations!

Praise the reader for the business accomplishment.

Most new businesses do not make it through their first year. For a business to flourish for 15 years is a great accomplishment. It is a testimony to your vision and dedication.

Express your expectation to do business with the firm in the future.

I hope we'll continue to be a part of your success in the future.

Reinforce your positive feelings.

Congratulations again! I know your next 15 years will be just as prosperous.

Use a friendly closing.

Cordially yours,

Best Wishes for the Holidays

Dear _____:

Explain the reason for this goodwill message.

During the busy year, we don't always have the opportunity to express our appreciation for the business we do together. But during the holiday season, we make sure our feelings are known.

Offer your best wishes and promise to continue to serve the customer well.

With our sincere holiday greetings and best wishes for a successful new year comes our thanks. Your loyalty and trust is the foundation upon which our business stands. We pledge to do everything in our power to maintain the standard of excellence you deserve in the coming year and beyond.

Convey your goodwill in a personal manner.

We hope that this holiday season brings you and your family health, happiness, and prosperity.

Use a friendly closing.

Cordially yours,

Best Wishes for a Marriage

Sincerely express your happiness at hearing the good news. (When writing a man, express your congratulations; for a woman, express your best wishes.)

Add a personal comment.

Close with a warm expression of your goodwill.

Use a friendly closing.

Note: If you have a personal as well as professional relationship with the addressee, you might want to mention that you look forward to meeting the spouse.

Dear _____:

I would like to convey my congratulations [best wishes] on your recent marriage. I was very happy to learn of this exciting event.

Although I do not know your spouse, I have heard wonderful things about her [him].

I wish both of you a lifetime of happiness together.

Cordially yours,

Best Wishes for a New Baby

Offer enthusiastic congratulations.

Make a positive, personal comment.

Use a friendly closing.

Note: If you have a personal as well as professional relationship with the addressee, you might mention that you look forward to "meeting the new addition to the family."

Dear _____:

Congratulations!

I was delighted to hear about the birth of your daughter. I can think of no more meaningful, joyous event in life than the birth of one's first child. I am so very happy for you.

My best wishes to all of you.

Cordially yours,

Sympathy for an Illness

Acknowledge the illness. If applicable, express your delight that all is going well. (If not, express your concern and hope that the reader recovers soon.)

Try to relieve the individual of some worry or concern.

Offer further assistance.

Wish the person well.

Use a friendly closing.

Dear _____:

I just heard about your emergency appendectomy. I was glad to learn, however, that all went well and you are recuperating.

During your recovery period, please promise me just two things. First, do not worry about the shipment of your pending orders. I will make sure the schedule is met. And second, get well soon!

If there is anything I can do to help, please let me know.

Wishing you a speedy recovery.

Cordially yours,

Sympathy for a Death— Close Associate

Dear _____:

Express your sincere sorrow.

I was shocked to hear about the unexpected death of your associate Arthur Crane. Please accept my deepest condolences.

Relate a favorable, personal incident or impression of the deceased.

I sold to Arthur for many years. Calling on Arthur was always a pleasure. He conducted business in a professional yet warm and friendly manner. He always got a big smile out of me with his wonderful sense of humor. I will really miss him.

Show your concern with an offer of assistance.

I understand that this is a difficult time for you. Please let me know if there is anything I can do to be of assistance.

Restate your condolences.

Again, my condolences to you.

Sincerely yours,

Note: In a case like this, a letter to the family would also be appropriate.

Sympathy for a Death—
Not a Close Associate

Dear _____:

Offer your sympathy.

I read in *Newsday* today of the loss of your brother, and I want to express my sincerest sympathy.

Make a caring, personal comment.

I want you to know that my thoughts are with you.

Restate your sympathy.

My deepest sympathy to you and your family.

Sincerely yours,

CHAPTER 7
LETTERS TO SALESPEOPLE

Sales managers constantly strive to motivate their sales forces. The difference between a successful and an ineffective sales team often is its level of motivation. Common strategies to motivate salespeople include personal pep talks, sales meetings, contests, and commission and bonus plans. In addition, sales managers employ sales letters to motivate their sales teams. A letter from a sales manager can be influential, as a point made in a letter often carries more weight than it would in conversation. Moreover, a sales letter is often the only effective way for a sales manager to communicate with sales forces in distant locations.

Letters to salespeople must be both *personal* and *positive*. The relationship of the sales manager to the salesperson is a personal one. Hence, all correspondence should be as individualized as possible. Form letters are particularly ineffective. Each salesperson wants to be recognized as a unique person with special needs and problems. The sooner a sales manager realizes this and incorporates personal anecdotes into letters, the more productive the letters will be. Here are some tips to help you keep your correspondence personal:

- Use the salesperson's first name in the body of the letter where appropriate.

- Before writing, picture the person with whom you are communicating.

- Write in a conversational style.

- Include references to the individual's family, hobbies, or interests.

- Let your natural personality and enthusiasm come through.

Letters to salespeople should be written from a positive perspective.

Even when a salesperson must be reprimanded, the letter should end on a note of positive expectation. Sales managers have seen that if they can communicate their confidence and expectation of success to their sales representatives, the salesperson is much more likely to succeed. Modern psychology calls this a "self-fulfilling prophecy." In other words, if a person believes he or she will be a success, that person will succeed. The sales manager's job is to ensure that the salespeople believe they will succeed. Letters that express a positive point of view help create a self-fulfilling prophecy of accomplishment and success.

Letter Congratulating a Salesperson on a Large Sale

Dear _____:

Open with enthusiastic congratulations.

Congratulations on your sale to Peterson Electric!

Praise the order.

It was the largest order we've had for the A801 Transducer this year.

Make a personal comment about the salesperson's effort.

I was particularly pleased with your sale because I know how hard you have worked with this account. I remember when we discussed Peterson and you told me how frustrating it was to call on them often, yet not see any movement.

I remember we both decided that, in this case, with the potential so great, it was worth the extra effort. Well, it certainly was!

Use this positive letter as an opportunity to state your expectation for future success. (When appropriate, reward the salesperson.)

I am confident that, with your positive attitude and willingness to go the extra mile, you will be a strong candidate for the number one sales representative here at Smith Electrical Supply. Keep up the fine work.

Restate your congratulations.

Congratulations again!

Sincerely yours,

Letter Congratulating a Salesperson for a Testimonial

Dear _____:

Offer congratulations.

Congratulations!

Explain the nature of the testimonial.

We have just received a letter from Interstate Van expressing their appreciation for the efficient and courteous service you have provided them.

Personally commend the achievement.

I know how demanding Interstate can be and recognize the significance of your achievement.

Reinforce the high standards of the company.

We are proud of the high level of service we at Acme provide. Your effort is a fine example of the excellence we strive for.

Enthusiastically reward the salesperson for the outstanding accomplishment.

We commend your positive attitude toward service. To express our delight in hearing this good news from such an important customer, we have enclosed a voucher for dinner for two at La Primavera.

Close by restating the congratulations.

Congratulations again, and keep up the excellent work.

Sincerely yours,

Letter Announcing a Change in Sales Policy

Dear _____:

State the price increase and the reason it is necessary.

On November 12, there will be a 10 percent price increase on all models of Contemporary Mahogany conference tables. This is due to the increase in labor costs for hand finishing.

Explain the increase in a positive manner.

While a price increase is not a selling point, it does represent our commitment to quality.

Comment on your commitment to quality products or services.

At Contemporary, we manufacture the finest office furniture available anywhere. We use rare, beautiful, natural woods from around the world. Old-world woodworkers handcraft each table individually. No two tables are ever the same; all are works of art.

Mention how the alternative to good quality would be unacceptable.

We could cut corners by using ordinary materials or by employing less skilled craftsmen, but then our tables would be like all the others . . . and not worthy of our name.

Offer a suggestion for overcoming an objection over price.

When making your sales presentation, do not be afraid of Contemporary's higher price. Instead, use it as a benefit by stressing the advantage of buying furniture of superior quality and design.

Cordially yours,

Letter Announcing a Sales Contest

Dear _____:

An intriguing question gets the salesperson involved.

Are you ready to pack your bags for an all-expenses-paid trip to beautiful Hawaii?

Announce the contest.

We sure hope so . . . since we're announcing Presto Copiers' Winter Getaway Vacation Sales Contest.

Motivate the entire sales force.

We want every one of our 325 sales representatives to win . . . and we've made it easy.

Give the details of the contest.

Here's how you can be a winner. Presto is launching a special promotion of the portable, CarryOn 2000 Personal Copier on November 1. The promotion will run until February 1. You only need to sell 15 machines in three months to win.

Express your expectation of success.

Since the CarryOn 2000 is the hottest photocopier we market and our advertising campaign is already producing leads, the sales goal will be a cinch to reach.

Describe the award to motivate the salesperson.

Here's the itinerary. You'll take a jumbo jet to Hawaii the first week in March. You'll check into a deluxe, ocean-view room at the renowned Hawaii Surf Club for seven fun-filled days. All your entertainment and dining will be arranged for you by the company. You'll see all the exciting sights and eat in the best restaurants. You can just relax and enjoy beautiful Hawaii.

Provide the details of the contest's kickoff.	Next week there will be a sales meeting to kick off this exciting contest. Until then, think Hawaii.
	Sincerely yours,
Use the postscript to further entice the salesperson by letting him or her know that the trip is attainable.	P.S. Last year 240 salespeople won the trip to Spain. This year, Hawaii is yours—if you want it!

Letter to Motivate a Salesperson

Dear _____:

Explain the positive reason for the letter.

I thought you'd be interested in a sales technique I learned from Bob Gray.

Start with a statement sure to spark interest. (If you do not have an in-house example, call on a famous or historical success story.)

I was amazed to see Bob Gray's sales for the last quarter. They were up 225 percent over the preceding quarter and 350 percent over the same quarter last year.

I quickly gave Bob a call to learn what he was doing. What Bob told me may help you get similar results.

Make the story interesting by keeping its tone personal. If possible, dramatize the story.

Bob said that two quarters ago his sales were flat—yet he was working as hard as ever. He was discouraged. So he sat down to analyze what he was doing. He took a piece of paper and listed all the active accounts and prospects he'd called on in the previous months. Then, using his sales diary to get the data, he drew a circle next to each account to represent each sales call he made. If the call resulted in a sale, he filled the circle in.

Bob was startled by what he discovered. There were many accounts where the circles were almost always filled in. There were other accounts where the circles were almost never filled in. And, in almost every case, if a circle was not filled in after two calls, it never got filled in.

Explain the lesson that was learned.

This meant that Bob was wasting two-thirds of his time calling again and again on accounts that, in all probability, would never order.

Show exactly how to apply the lesson to the reader's daily sales routine.	Bob immediately changed his approach to selling. He gave every new prospect just two chances (calls) to order. After that, he placed them on his mailing list but made no more sales calls to them. Bob concentrated on servicing "ordering accounts," and on calling on more and more <u>new</u> prospects. But the new prospects got only two sales calls.
Enthusiastically state the benefit.	Bob's sales began to soar. He was using his time and effort where it would pay off and had stopped spinning his wheels with prospects that would never order.
Tell the salesperson what must be done to improve sales.	You can do what Bob did. Analyze whether your selling time is being spent as productively.
Reinforce the benefit.	The answer could help you increase your sales 225 percent or more!
	Sincerely yours,

Letter to Motivate a Salesperson with a Morale Problem

Dear _____:

Calmly state the problem.

It has come to my attention that your sales volume has sharply decreased over the last quarter.

Express your surprise that the problem has developed.

This surprises me, as you have always been among the very best salespeople here at Norton-Perkins.

Describe your positive expectation that the problem will be solved.

I am surprised, but not upset. I say this because I truly believe that once you've been successful in sales, you can easily be successful again. And knowing you as I do, I am confident you will soon be on top once more.

Make a constructive suggestion.

When Jack Nicklaus, the greatest golfer of all time, finds himself in a slump (and he has), he does something that makes a great deal of sense. He goes back to basics. He looks at the fundamentals of his game: his grip, stance, backswing, etc. Maybe going back to basics can work for you.

Focus on a positive quality of the salesperson and give enthusiastic praise.

I have always thought your superior ability in sales resulted from your enthusiasm for the product and real concern for helping the customer. These two factors, along with your desire to be successful, are your "basics."

Why not take a good, hard look at your enthusiasm for the product, your concern for the customer, and desire for success. If any of these areas needs work, commit yourself to it.

Reinforce your expectation that the problem will be solved.	It may take a month or two, but I know your sales will improve dramatically.

Don't be discouraged. Do what Jack Nicklaus does. Go back to basics. |
| Offer personal assistance, if required. | If you want to meet with me, just give me a call.

Sincerely yours, |

CHAPTER 8

LETTERS TO SELL YOURSELF

Letters that sell your ideas and talents can be difficult ones to write. The reason for this is the possibility that your letter may sound boastful and self-serving rather than confident and believable. To convince the prospect of your reliability, your letters must be *personal, sincere, positive,* and *credible.*

A letter can be called *personal* when it is written as if you were talking directly to the recipient. Picture the person you are writing to and avoid thinking of the individual as a "market."

Sincerity is expressed by revealing or giving something of yourself to the reader. It could be honest appreciation for the opportunity to describe your idea or an earnest offer of assistance.

Whatever form it takes, sincerity is necessary for your letter to be effective.

To sell yourself, you must first believe in yourself and your ability to provide the reader with the benefit promised. A *positive,* enthusiastic approach will assure the prospect of your confidence and make your argument hard to resist.

The reader has probably never heard of you and needs evidence of your talent. You can establish your *credibility* by citing credentials, education, experience, and references.

By using these influential factors in letters that sell yourself, you will avoid exaggeration and pie-in-the-sky promises. You'll find people will believe what you say and respond with interest.

Letter Requesting a Job Interview

Dear _____ :

Express your knowledge and interest in the potential employer.

I have been an office systems salesperson for over 10 years, and I have watched the growth of your company closely. I am very impressed with your aggresive approach to product development and with the strong support you give your sales personnel.

State why you are seeking a job change.

I am looking for a new, more challenging position in sales with a company like yours.

Confidently inform the employer of your qualifications.

If you are seeking a salesperson with a proven track record and the desire and motivation to excel, then I believe I can be an asset to your organization.

Substantiate your claims with evidence.

The enclosed resume describes some of my accomplishments. You'll notice that for the last five years I have ranked within the top three sales representatives in my company. On two occasions, I have achieved the number one position.

Predict your future success with a new company. Request a meeting with the prospective emplyer.

I know that I can produce great results for you. I will call you next week to see if we can meet.

Sincerely yours,

Letter Answering an Employment Advertisement

Dear _____:

State the reason why you are writing.

As an advertising manager for a food distributor, I feel fully qualified for the position with Appropriate Foods that you listed in the April 23 issue of the *New York Times*.

Make a positive presentation of your qualifications.

My 14 years' experience with companies in the food industry has provided me with hands-on knowledge of every aspect of sales promotion and advertising in your industry. I know that I can use my talents to help your company grow and profit.

Discuss your resume and point out specific accomplishments.

I have enclosed my resume for you to consider. You'll notice that I have won three consecutive Alpha Awards for excellence in the category of food promotion.

Ask for a meeting. Mention an extra reason to meet if possible.

I would greatly appreciate the opportunity to meet with you to discuss my qualifications in relation to your needs. At that time you'll be able to review my portfolio.

Tell when the employer should expect your call.

I will call you next Thursday morning to see if we can set up an appointment at your convenience.

Sincerely yours,

Letter Asking for a Consulting Job

Dear _____:

Begin with a statement that the prospect will find interesting.

There is probably no more challenging occupation than running a small family business.

Acknowledge a common problem.

The owner of a family business has to overcome not only the multitude of problems facing every business person trying to run a successful business, but also the confusing emotional problems of working with one's family.

Develop the problem further.

Most family business owners have no problem making business decisions, but struggle when decisions regarding the family and the business are necessary.

Describe what you can do to solve the problem.

That's where I can help you. Not only have I run a successful family business, but I have studied and worked with hundreds of them. As a family business consultant, I understand your needs. I can help you decide what makes sense for you, your business, and your family.

Mention specific problem areas where you can be of help.

I can help you with problem areas such as responsibilities, compensation, tax planning, and succession.

Describe a significant benefit as a result of solving the problem.

It is common to see companies begin to grow significantly once these issues are finally resolved.

Explain what action you will take.

I will call you next week to see if we can set up a meeting to discuss your special situation. I look forward to talking with you.

Sincerely yours,

Letter Offering to Give a Seminar

Headline excites interest and ties in directly with perceived need.

CREATIVITY CAN BE LEARNED

Dear _____:

Open with a direct statement of your proposal and its benefits.

I believe I can provide Management Methods Seminars with a program on creativity in business that would be extremely profitable to you and beneficial to your students.

Build credibility with a description of your experience.

For the last 20 years, I have served as vice president of product development for three Fortune 500 companies, and I am now the president of my own product firm, PRD Development.

I have presented a creativity seminar for many of my clients, and the reaction has always been excellent.

Show the need for the seminar.

My clients all agreed that every business needs a constant flow of creative ideas in order to stay ahead of the competition. But unfortunately, creative people are in short supply.

Answer the need with your proposal.

I helped these clients realize that we are all born with the ability to be creative! My program shows, in a practical, step-by-step manner, how every one of us can be in touch with our natural creative talent. Using examples from my many years of experience, I will show participants how to apply new creative thinking to their businesses. Each attendee will leave the program with the tools necessary to be more spontaneous, innovative, and creative.

Positively state your expectation of success.

I know you'll find this program to be a valuable addition to Management Methods Seminars.

Tell the reader what to expect next.

I'll call you next week to see if we can set up a meeting to discuss my proposal.

Sincerely yours,

Letter of Invitation for an Opening

Dear _____:

Warmly extend the invitation.

I am very pleased to invite you to the opening of my new gallery/studio. The opening will begin at 6:00 P.M. on the evening of June 22 at 110 Artisan Way.

Sincerely describe the importance of the event. Give thanks for past patronage.

This is a very special occasion for me. As you know, I have always dreamed of opening a gallery. And thanks to loyal support from friends like you, this day has become a reality.

Promote the exhibition.

On display will be an exciting new series of watercolors depicting the beautiful New England seacoast.

State your positive expectation of the guest's attendance.

I look forward to seeing you on June 22 and showing you my new work.

Sincerely yours,

The postscript suggests an additional benefit of attending.

P.S. Refreshments will be served.

Letter Selling an Idea

Dear _____:

Open with a sincere expression of admiration.

I may be your greatest fan!

Show your knowledge of and interest in the prospect's business.

As a board game enthusiast, I own over 200 board games from various manufacturers. Two of yours, Spy and Shipwrecked, are my favorites.

Get right to the point and describe your idea. Be enthusiastic.

I have just developed a game I believe you'll want to see. It is a game lover's game, yet it appeals to a far wider audience. "Count and Counterpoint" is a game of wit and strategy. It can be played alone or by two to six people. Once play is begun, the player is lost in the excitement and challenge of matching intelligence and cunning with his or her opponents.

Express how your idea will benefit the company. Propose a short, pressure-free meeting.

Once you see and play Count and Counterpoint, you'll appreciate its fantastic potential in the game market. But you be the judge. All I need is 10 minutes of your time.

Tell the prospect exactly what you intend to do next.

I will call you next Wednesday to see if I can set up a convenient time to present Count and Counterpoint to you.

Sincerely yours,

CHAPTER 9

SERIAL LETTERS

A serial-letter sales campaign consists of a series of letters sent at regular intervals to the same customer or prospect.

Serial letters are particularly effective for selling products or services that require extensive explanation, description, or promotion. The multiple-letter format provides an ongoing give and take through which a substantial sales case can be built. Often a product or service has many exciting features. The serial letter gives you the opportunity to explain each one fully. You also avoid confusing the reader with many different sales points in one letter.

By presenting many sales messages, you are able to find and appeal to the prospect's "hot button." If, for example, you were selling custom men's suits, you could send a different letter for each of the following sales features:

- Choice of fabric
- Personal attention
- Factory-direct prices
- Custom fitting
- Guarantee
- Style
- Convenience
- Expert tailoring
- Lifetime alterations
- Silk lining

One prospect might buy after the first letter, another after the sixth, and it might take all ten letters to interest still others. The prospect who always wanted a suit with a silk lining is not prodded to action until the tenth letter. If only the first letter had been sent to this prospect, his "hot button" might never have been pushed.

When creating a serial-letter campaign, always assume the reader will not remember your previous letter or letters. While many readers will remember, a great many will not. And letters often get lost or are tossed away unread. Therefore, each letter should stand on its own, as if it were the only letter to be sent. By keeping this in mind, you assure that each letter presents a strong, complete sales argument.

First Letter—Selling Price

Dear Mr. Elliot:

Capture interest with an intriguing statement.	<u>You may be paying much more than you should for business envelopes.</u>
Suggest how the reader can save money.	That's because most envelope suppliers are jobbers and not manufacturers.
Present the benefit of buying from you.	Direct Envelope Inc. is an envelope manufacturer. And, because you buy directly from us, you can save 30 percent, 40 percent, and even 50 percent off what you're now paying.
Create credibility with a printed price list.	Hard to believe? Let me prove it to you. I've enclosed a copy of our regular price list with this letter. Check our prices against your last invoice for envelopes. I guarantee you're paying more for the same product. Don't you think you should place your next order with Direct Envelope?
Make a special offer.	To help convince you to give us a try, we'll help you save even more on your first order. Mark your order "first-time customer," and Direct Envelope will pay all shipping and handling charges.
Tell the reader what action to take.	Return the postage-paid order card today and take advantage of the factory-direct prices and special, "first-order" offer.

Sincerely yours,

Second Letter—Selling Service

Dear Mr. Elliot:

Try an opening statement that leaves a question in the reader's mind, thereby building interest.

I'd like to tell you something you may already know . . . and something that may surprise you.

Continue the theme of the opening sentence by describing the first benefit.

You may be aware that you can save up to 50 percent off what you are currently paying for business envelopes by buying directly from Direct Envelope Inc.

Introduce the second benefit of excellent service.

What may surprise you is that you'll realize those savings and get better service at the same time!

Explain how you provide better service.

It's true. When you order envelopes from most suppliers, they take your order and send it on to the manufacturer. Two parties are involved.

When you buy from Direct Envelope, your order goes straight to us. You benefit in two ways. First, you save time. In most cases we can ship your order to you within 72 hours. Second, you have better control. Without a third party involved, there's less chance an error will be made.

Direct the customer to take action.

A handy price list and direct order card are enclosed with this letter. Order now and see for yourself that you can get excellent service and pay a reasonable price.

Describe the special offer.

If you mark your order "first-time customer," Direct Envelope will pay all shipping and handling charges. You can't lose, so please place your order today.

Sincerely yours,

Third Letter—Selling Selection

Dear Mr. Elliot:

A challenging statement grabs the reader's attention.	I bet the last time you ordered business envelopes, you ordered them in white.
Establish a benefit of your product. (Here, the writer provides information that the prospect will find valuable.)	Did you know that colored envelopes get opened sooner and are less likely to be thrown out unopened than white envelopes?
Present the benefit of a large selection.	We're Direct Envelope Inc., and we sell white envelopes as well as envelopes in buff, ivory, rose, peach, yellow, goldenrod, green, blue, red, pink, gray, silver, and 15 other eye-catching colors. Each color is manufactured in eight envelope sizes. This represents the largest variety of envelopes available anywhere. Now you can order every color and size you need from one convenient source.
Add a second benefit.	As you may already know, we manufacture these envelopes and sell them to you directly— without any middleman. With us, you can save up to 50 percent on what you would normally pay.
Make a special offer.	I've enclosed our price list, color chart, and order card. Mark your first order "first-time customer," and we'll pay all shipping and handling charges. It's our way of thanking you for your order and welcoming you as a new customer.

Ask for the order.

Please send in your order card today and take advantage of the everyday low prices and special first-order offer.

Sincerely yours,

Fourth Letter—Selling One Product in the Line

Dear Mr. Elliot:

Use a sample to gain interest. If no sample is available, use a picture, data sheet, or other illustration.

<u>Take a good look at the sample mailing envelope enclosed. You've probably never seen anything like it!</u>

Promise a powerful benefit.

Now you can double the effectiveness of your mailings with the new QuickReply Mailing Envelope from Direct Envelope Inc.

Explain how the product delivers the promised benefit.

This remarkable, cost-effective mailing format has been tested and shown to increase response. That's because it's so easy for the receiver to open and return. The envelope almost says "mail me back."

Describe the product.

The QuickReply Envelope's features include:

- Three foldout panels for your advertising message
- A perforated, tear-off business reply card
- An intriguing pull tab to open the envelope
- Ample space for an address and sales message
- Availability in five attention-getting colors
- Many other sales-boosting features

Suggest how the reader can benefit by using the product.

You can use QuickReply to market a wide variety of products and services. Your imagination is your only limitation.

Tell the reader how to get more information.

To find out how this dynamic new marketing vehicle can sell your product, return the reply card or call us today.

Sincerely yours,

Offer information on other products. This may appeal to a reader who is not interested in the special product.

P.S. When you respond, we'll send you FREE details on Direct Envelope's extensive line of envelopes—the largest selection available anywhere!

Fifth Letter—Selling Reputation

Dear Mr. Elliot:

<u>My father would never buy from my company, and I consider him an excellent businessman!</u>

He wouldn't purchase a single business envelope from his son's company, Direct Envelope Inc., until he was satisfied with the answer to a question he asked all potential suppliers.

What was the question that this veteran purchasing agent always asked? "Who's been buying from you for five years or more and what are their names and telephone numbers?"

My father, you see, was very wise. He had learned the hard way that you could go to the bank on a company's reputation.

We want you to go to the bank on our reputation. We've worked long and hard to become one of the most respected envelope manufacturers in the country. And we'd like you to be absolutely confident about our dedication to providing you with a quality product and excellent service at a competitive price.

I have attached to this letter a list of companies that we've been proud to serve for at least five

Capture attention with an intriguing statement.

Build upon the interest created with a personal story. (Other alternatives are to cite case histories of particular clients, or unusual incidents where your company saved the day.)

Relate the story to your company. Show how you have earned a good reputation.

Build credibility with evidence of your reliability.

Close with a positive expectation of future business.

years. Please call any or all of them. Ask them the questions my father would ask. Then buy from Direct Envelope with confidence.

I look forward to serving you in the future.

Sincerely yours,

CHAPTER 10
NOVELTY LETTERS

A novelty letter is a letter designed to gain the reader's attention with unique formats or enclosures. Novelty letters are often effective and can raise the level of response significantly. However, novelty letters are not suited to every situation and, if used inappropriately, can create disastrous results. The danger in using novelty letters is in alienating the audience by being too cute or gimmicky. Also, once you've used a novelty letter with a client, be sure your subsequent mailings use new approaches. Nothing is as much of a turn-off as an overused novelty format.

An example of a novelty format is the telegram look-alike letter. Generally printed in bright yellow, the envelope and letterhead are purposely fashioned after a telegram or mailgram. Bold print on the envelope reads "urgent," "important," or "dated material." The format gives the impression that the letter is of consequence and should be opened immediately. If the "telegram" actually contains a telegram-worthy message such as a limited-time offer, introductory sale, or closeout of merchandise, the letter may be effective. But if the offer is not of special value, the prospect may be annoyed.

Common enclosures in novelty letters are printed specialties and miniature objects. Some examples of these include:

- Pictures
- Adhesive discount labels
- Treasure maps
- Quizzes
- Coins
- Charms
- Pens and pencils

- Model vehicles
- Pop-up figures
- Toys

It is extremely important that the enclosure tie in with the product or service being sold. Recently, an excellent tie-in crossed my desk. A company that sells industrial cleansers included a picture of an orange in a mailing. The orange was saturated with an orange fragrance that was used in a new washroom cleanser. One could not open the mailing and avoid smelling the orange fragrance. The sales letter's message was "have your washrooms smelling like fresh oranges." The sample fragrance was an effective tie-in.

An example of a tie-in enclosure that missed the mark was sent by a company selling mortgage services. They included a telephone book in their solicitation. No connection between their service and the enclosure was apparent. A better enclosure would have been an amortization chart with their name and phone number imprinted. They could have asked the reader to "Check out our low, low mortgage rates on the handy chart."

Here is one last caution on using novelty letter formats and enclosures. Always make sure that the attention-getting device does not interfere with the reason for the letter: to generate sales. The novelty letter, like any sales letter, must induce the prospect to order, request information, ask for a demonstration, visit a store, or take an action that leads to a sale. Remember, a novelty letter with a great interest-building format or enclosure must still entice the reader, provide product information, create a desire to buy, and tell the reader how to order.

Aspirin Letter

Two aspirin are attached to the letter to capture the reader's attention.

Dear _____:

If finding a reliable office-cleaning service gives you a headache, take two of these . . .

and call me in the morning!

It's unfortunate, but most office cleaners are unreliable.

You get your office ready for cleaning . . .
and they don't show up.
You tell them what to clean . . .
and they forget to clean it.
You ask them to be careful . . .
and you find things broken.
You insist on honesty . . .
and items disappear.
You demand that the office be thoroughly cleaned . . .
and it's still dirty.

We will cure your office-cleaning "headaches."

How? It starts at the top. I began Spotless after many years as a corporate executive because I saw a need for a professional office-cleaning business. I know how to run a business in which nothing matters except excellent service and the customer's satisfaction. Spotless provides you with the service you've always wanted. We refuse to tolerate mediocrity.

To find out how easy it is to have your office cleaned quickly and professionally, call Spotless today. The last thing you'll get from us is a headache!

Sincerely yours,

P.S. Ask about our FREE first visit!

Mirror Letter

A small mirror attached to the letter generates curiosity.

Dear _____:

"Mirror, mirror on the wall . . . who is the fairest of them all?"

It can be you if you use Nature Perfect Wrinkle-Away Cream.

Wrinkle-Away is a unique blend of nature's most beautifying moisturizers, including peanut oil, olive oil, almond oil, lanolin, PABA, and vitamin E. As you massage Wrinkle-Away into your skin, dryness and wrinkles disappear You feel your skin tingle as it is miraculously revitalized right before your eyes. Your skin actually recaptures the smoothness and luster of youth.

Look in the mirror we sent you. Are you satisfied with the youthfulness of your skin? If not, order a 30-day supply of Wrinkle-Away at our special introductory price of $19.95. That's a savings of $10.00 off the regular price.

Use Wrinkle-Away for a full week. Then look in the mirror again. If your skin does not appear many years younger, return the remaining supply for a full refund.

Don't take my word for it—see for yourself!

Return the handy order form today with your check for only $19.95. Take advantage of this introductory offer. You'll be glad you did.

Sincerely yours,

Upside-Down Letter

Print the letter upside-down on letterhead stationery as an attention-getting device.

Dear _____:

DO YOU EVER FEEL THE WORLD IS TURNED UPSIDE DOWN?

Most of us do at one time or another. That's because in today's fast-paced society, tremendous demands are put on us. The stress of earning a living and raising a family can make one's head spin.

Luckily, I've found a simple way to reduce stress and put my feet back on the ground. How? By using the WellBeing Relaxation System. Every day I spend 20 quiet minutes doing relaxation exercises that calm me both physically and psychologically. When I'm through I feel refreshed and revitalized. The anxieties and problems of the day don't seem nearly as overwhelming. I feel at ease and in control.

Doctors say that everyone can benefit from a daily relaxation routine. Psychologists concur.

Don't you think you owe it to yourself to investigate this inexpensive, enjoyable program?

I'd like to send you a FREE audio cassette that explains the WellBeing Relaxation System and includes a sample relaxation exercise. Try it for yourself and see how good it makes you feel.

It's time to put your world right side up, and we're ready to prove everything we claim with our FREE cassette. So, mail the coupon or call us today!

Sincerely yours,

P.S. The WellBeing program, used during the day, helps you sleep better at night. It has cured many insomniacs!

Two-Sided Letter

Dear _____:

This letter has two sides.

THIS IS OUR "SIDE."   THIS IS YOUR "SIDE."

Quite a long time has passed since your last order, and we are very concerned.

When a loyal customer like you stops ordering from us, it is both bad and good. Bad because we value your friendship and business greatly and would never wish to lose your trust. Good because it allows us to see where we may have fallen short and permits us to correct our mistakes.

The success of our company depends entirely upon the satisfaction of our customers and nothing else. If we have erred, we apologize and hope there is a way we can make it up to you.

Please use your "side" of this letter to jot down exactly why we no longer have your business. Be as candid as you want.

Won't you send your "side" to us soon? The faster we receive your answer, the faster we can begin to serve you better. We've enclosed a postage-paid reply envelope for your convenience.

Sincerely yours,

Letter with an Unusual Layout

Dear _____:

ARE
   YOU
      WATCHING
         THE
            VALUE
               OF
                  YOUR
                     INVESTMENTS
                     GOING
                        DOWN
                          DOWN
                            DOWN?

We'd like to show you a SAFE way to achieve steady financial growth of your investments and reach your financial goals without risk.

Bradley and Bradley has been advising investors just like you since 1910. We investigate the marketplace to discover opportunities for your money to grow safely. Our prudent, responsible approach to investing will help you realize the security you want in your future.

Currently, we are recommending a U.S. government security mutual fund. This fund has performed strongly over the last three years, returning an average of 12 percent. The forecast for the next 12 months is excellent.

To learn how you can take advantage of this and other SAFE investments, call us today.

Sincerely yours,

P.S. Wouldn't it be nice to see your investments go up for a change?

Letter with Marginal Notations

Dear Friend:

You can shed weight fast and easily with the revolutionary Fiberoff Plan.

Not a Diet!

We call it a plan and not a diet because with Fiberoff you never feel like you're dieting. You naturally begin to eat less because you never feel hungry.

Better yet, the Fiberoff Plan is:

Most Important!

- Perfectly safe

- Easy to follow

- Inexpensive

- Guaranteed

Thousands have tried Fiberoff and have reached their weight goals without hunger. Now you can too!

Here's what typical Fiberoff weight losers are saying:

- "The only diet that's ever worked for me."
  B. Harris

- "I lost 12 pounds during the first week!"
  R. Denver

● "I turned all my friends on to Fiberoff after I lost 22 pounds." T. Jamesway

All you do is take four Fiberoff tablets half an hour before mealtime. That's it!

Fiberoff immediately starts to work in two ways.

First, it makes you feel less hungry. Your actual desire to eat wanes.

Second, the natural, high-fiber ingredients in Fiberoff quicken the digestive process. Food actually passes through your body twice as fast as normal. Your body eliminates calories it would normally absorb.

Works Scientifically!

With Fiberoff, you eat just as you did before. After a few days, you'll find that your yen for sweets and snacks disappears. You'll be eating less and yet feel satisfied with three light meals a day. You won't want to eat as much!

You Won't Feel Hungry!

As a special intoduction to the Fiberoff Plan, we offer you your first week's supply of Fiberoff FREE. Here's what you do:

Order your first month's supply now. We'll immediately rush you your order, an informative guide book, and an extra week's supply of Fiberoff, FREE.

Use your free sample first. Let Fiberoff prove to you its amazing weight loss power before you use any of the month's supply.

Ironclad Guarantee!

If you do not lose _more_ weight faster than ever before, or are unhappy for any reason, return the month's supply for a full refund. Could anything be fairer?

Please send in the order card today. Remember, it only takes one week to begin to see the pounds melt away.

Sincerely yours,

A Sexier You!

P.S. Start the Fiberoff Plan now, and you'll be wearing sexy swimsuits by summer!

Additional Tips: Salutations

The salutation is one of the most important elements in any letter, as it is the first thing the reader sees. This list may help you to think of the best way to get your prospect or client's interest.

Dear Valued Customer:
Dear Friend:
Dear Vacationer:
Dear Animal Lover:
Dear Reader:
Dear Neighbor:
Dear Bostonian:
Dear Member:
Dear Applicant:
Dear Skier:
Dear Opportunity Seeker:
Dear Good Friend:

Dear Friend and Customer:
Dear Direct Marketer:
Dear Advertising Manager:
Dear Business Owner:
Dear Sales Professional:
Dear Contributor:
Dear Retailer:
Dear Patron:
Welcome:
Hello:
Good Morning:
Greetings:
Enclosed:
Just for you . . .
You're about to learn . . .
For you only . . .
You are invited to . . .

Words for Headlines

These are high-powered words that instantly draw and hold the reader's attention.

Now
New
Free
Announcing
Best
Breakthrough
Unlimited
Wealth
Money
Happiness
Amazing
Revolutionary
Improved
Latest
Top Secret
Confidential
Discover
Revealed
Treasure
Sexy
Powerful
Limited
Opportunity

Offer
Ultimate
Millionaire
Famous
Attention
Fact
Imagine
Gigantic
True
Don't
Stop
Perfect
Easy
Save
Great
Terrific
Important
Value
Approved
Practical
Safe
Help
Unique
Handy
Fast
Instantly

Transitions That Work

Effective transitions, always important in good writing, are especially important in sales letters, as they ensure that the addressee continues reading. Here are a few suggestions:

The answer is . . .
Here's what happened . . .
In addition, . . .
It's even better than that!
Here's why:
And there's more good news!
It's true!
To say it in another way, . . .
More than that, . . .
Better still, . . .
Happily, . . .
Last but not least, . . .

And don't forget, . . .
For more information, . . .
Read on!
There's more!
Too good to be true?
Consider this:
All that and _____ too!
How can this benefit you?
What's in it for you?
Don't take my word for it, . . .
Why is this important?
Best of all, . . .
Would you like to hear more?
That's not all!
More important, . . .
To reiterate, . . .
To say it in another way, . . .

Openings

The decision on whether or not to read a letter is often based on the letter's first few lines, so make sure they're attention-getting or provocative. Some ideas are:

Think for a moment about the people you know who are successful . . . what do they all have in common?

If you think you can get rich working for someone else, you're dead wrong!

Earn more money than you ever dreamed possible.

You are 1 in 100,000!

We're still waiting to hear from you.

Could you use an extra $200 a week?

Your interest in our offer is greatly appreciated.

What will you be doing in the year 2000?

How secure will you be 10 years from now?

Here's a money-making opportunity I know you'll want to learn about.

This exclusive insider's information is offered to a select few!

Do you believe in miracles?

Turn your wildest dreams into reality.

Don't read another word if you're satisfied with your present income.

Have you ever dreamed about owning your own home?

We have reserved a FREE copy of _____ for you.

Take a minute from your busy schedule to read this letter . . . you will not regret it.

It's been three weeks since I sent you the information you requested on refinancing your home, and I haven't heard from you.

The survey is in, and the results may startle you.

If you are over 55 and do not read *Maturity Today* magazine, you may be unprepared for the years ahead.

Spend $25 today and earn $1,000 tomorrow.

If you can answer this question correctly, you may have a career in computer programming.

Did anyone ever tell you that you missed your true calling?

You are cordially invited to join the Inner Circle Theater Club as a charter member.

You have been recommended for membership in a select society.

The discount ticket enclosed entitles you to a 20 percent savings on Thompson Lawn Care products.

Until now, this offer could not be made.

Take the first step toward financial security.

Because of your keen desire to succeed, we offer you this amazing opportunity.

Have you ever heard of a "win-win" situation?

Your friend, Tim Connors, has given your name and asked that I write you.

Do you want to be your own boss?

The following question has only one correct answer.

Most people cannot answer this riddle.

There are four secrets to success, and you already possess three of them.

Reliable service is not a thing of the past.

We would like to take this opportunity to wish you a Happy New Year and thank you for your past patronage.

Your subscription expires soon.

I recently wrote you about an important opportunity.

Did you ever wish you could do something entirely different?

The opportunity you've been waiting for has just arrived.

If I had known what I am about to tell you, my life would have been very different.

Your Rolls Royce may be being built now!

You can be a hero to your company.

You can now join a select group of _____.

Take this challenge and realize your dreams.

Don't read this unless _____.

We would like to offer you a ground-floor opportunity.

Your free trial issue of _____ is enclosed, as well as information on a special offer.

If I told you that investing just one hour a night for the next 30 days could double your income, would you believe me?

Our value-packed holiday sale lasts only five days.

I am going to tell you about an incident that changed my life.

Here are the product sheets you requested.

Can we talk man to man [woman to woman]?

Your name has been selected at random.

I personally invite you to _____.

The three minutes it takes to read this letter could change your life.

Announcing a breakthrough in _____ technology!

You can be among the first to learn about _____.

Tired of _____ that never work?

Are you concerned about your family's safety?

It's brand new!

Are you a person who likes to take risks?

Psst . . . Here is a sure winner.

Can you be sure your business will survive the changing times ahead?

You demand quality . . . and we guarantee it!

Don't gamble with your family's future.

You are about to make a very important decision.

The _____ you've been waiting for is finally here!

This may sound like a silly question.

May I ask for a few moments of your valuable time?

It will only take 66 seconds to read this letter.

Yours to try FREE for 15 days . . . this extraordinary, portable personal computer.

I'm still waiting to hear from you.

A few months ago you inquired about having your house painted.

How business-smart are you?

I'm asking you today for your continued support of _____ in 1988.

The secret report enclosed can change your life.

Closings

The closing is your last chance to clinch a sale. Make it strong and active; you want to move the reader to respond. Consider:

Because of the limited number of _____ available, we advise you to consider this opportunity now.

Don't miss out on the upcoming action-packed issue of _____.

Your immediate attention will start you on your way to greater success.

If you have any questions, please call and ask to speak to me.

We'll rush your order as soon as we receive your reply.

You will not be disappointed.

You'll see, it's even better than you imagine.

Drop the reply card in the mail today!

Don't hesitate—act now!

Just mail the enclosed reply card for your no-obligation information kit.

I have reserved your free gift, but to redeem it you must act now.

By renewing for two years now, you save $18 off the year-by-year renewal rate. It's like getting a full year FREE.

A year from now you'll be very glad you did.

Take my word for it. You'll be more than pleased.

Call now to arrange a no-obligation demonstration.

Take advantage of this one-time offer.

To speed your order, call _____ now!

Your reply will be held in strictest confidence.

You have seven days to take advantage of this opportunity.

Send in the application, and we'll process it immediately.

You've got nothing to lose and much to gain.

Act now while the special offer is still in effect.

When you are ready to order, we will be pleased to help you.

It's our pleasure to serve you.

We greatly appreciate your continued business.

I promise, you won't be sorry.

I personally guarantee it.

You will never again see _____ at a price this low.

You owe it to yourself to give it a try.

Your family will really appreciate it.

Please phone us now—a representative will be waiting for your call.

Time is running out, so order today!

If for any reason you are not totally satisfied, return it for a "no-questions-asked" refund.

The 30-day trial offer guarantees there is no risk to you.

Renew your subscription today to ensure uninterrupted delivery.

Won't you call me now?

Take this important step today.

Take this giant step now.

Remember, this offer will not be made again.

Try it. I know you'll be delighted.

Remember, our guarantee takes away all risk.

All you need to do to get started is to return the reply card.

Fifty thousand have already ordered. Now you can, too!

Check off the plan that best suits your needs.

Protect your family's financial future with this intelligent investment.

Don't you agree that it's time to take this important step?

If you have any questions regarding a tax or financial matter, please feel free to call us at any time.

No need to send money now; we'll bill you later.

It's up to you to take advantage of this "win-win" situation.

If you are not completely satisfied, simply write "cancel" on your invoice and return it to me.

There is still time if you act now.

You'll be surprised at how easy it is to afford.

If you don't decide to do it now, you'll miss a great opportunity.

Send no money; you will be billed later.

The decision is entirely in your hands.

Call our toll-free number. Our friendly operators will be happy to assist you.

Don't you think it's worth investigating?

Order your copy of _____ now, before the _____ deadline.

Remember to order soon to stock up before next month's price increase!

Don't wait. Start taking advantage of _____'s money-saving features today!

This unusual offer comes to you just once, so order now!

Complete and mail the form now.

So make the winning decision this moment.

Years from now, you'll look back on this decision as one of the wisest you ever made.

This offer is good only until the date shown on your acceptance form.

For fastest action, call us at _____.

If, after using your car cover for 15 days, you are not convinced of its value, ignore our invoice, return the car cover, and owe nothing.

Call me to discuss how we can give you the quality you demand.

So please, don't be a stranger . . . let us know how you are and how we can help you.

ORDER NOW FOR YOUR PERFECT COMPANION TO *LETTERS THAT SELL*